Best Management Practice
Portfolio Product

D1401404

ITIL® Lite
A road map to full or partial ITIL implementation

London: TSO

Published by TSO (The Stationery Office) and available from:

Online
www.tsoshop.co.uk

Mail, Telephone, Fax & E-mail
TSO
PO Box 29, Norwich, NR3 1GN
Telephone orders/General enquiries: 0870 600 5522
Fax orders: 0870 600 5533
E-mail: customer.services@tso.co.uk
Textphone: 0870 240 3701

TSO@Blackwell and other Accredited Agents

A CIP catalogue record for this book is available from the British Library
A Library of Congress CIP catalogue record has been applied for

First edition 2010
Second edition 2012

First published 2012

ISBN 9780113313839

Printed in the United Kingdom by The Stationery Office, London

P002509608   c8   10/12

Contents

List of figures and tables

FIGURES

TABLES

Preface

ITIL® Lite is an approach to implementing key ITIL components to provide a sound basis for IT service management – either as a starting point for full implementation or as a deliverable for those not wishing to fully implement ITIL.

The ITIL core consists of five publications:

- *ITIL Service Strategy*
- *ITIL Service Design*
- *ITIL Service Transition*
- *ITIL Service Operation*
- *ITIL Continual Service Improvement.*

Each publication is also a phase in the service lifecycle. The ITIL 2011 editions were published by The Stationery Office in July 2011.

Two common questions seem to arise when discussing ITIL implementation with service management professionals. Firstly, where is the starting point for implementing ITIL? Secondly, is it necessary to implement the whole of ITIL? Note that the questions were not *should* we implement ITIL, but *how* should we implement it.

Before discussing how to implement ITIL Lite it is important to explain the reasoning and logic behind the concept. It is not meant to compete with, or in any way denigrate, ITIL. It has been created to assist those organizations that are adopting, or thinking of adopting, ITIL. There are many organizations that, for different reasons (see section 1.1), cannot or will not be implementing ITIL in its entirety. There are also those organizations that are looking towards full ITIL implementation but are confused as to where to start this journey. ITIL Lite is aimed at both of these groups.

ABOUT THIS PUBLICATION

In essence, this is a practical guide to building a plan to successfully implement ITIL Lite. Its step-by-step approach will reduce the time required to create an ITIL project.

This publication provides a good basic understanding of how the various ITIL components can be linked and integrated in a logical and structured manner. It supplements and extends the traditional sources of ITIL education and helps to quantify the view of ITIL as a complete service, and not a series of numerous components.

The chapters are colloquial and conversational in tone. This is intentional – the steps are easier to explain in this way, and easier for you to remember.

WHO SHOULD READ THIS PUBLICATION?

This publication is aimed at a wide audience, from those who are trying to decide whether to implement ITIL to those who are actively looking to build an ITIL project. It will help guide those managing the project and give project team members a valuable insight into how their ITIL Lite project is constructed. In fact, anyone who has any role to play in ITIL implementation will find this publication valuable and, because ITIL touches upon many parts of IT, even non-ITSM professionals may want to understand how they could be affected by it (they will find Chapter 3 on categorization particularly interesting).

1

Why ITIL Lite?

1 Why ITIL Lite?

There are 26 processes and four functions (see Figure 1.1) described in the ITIL 2011 editions. ITIL is a framework and not a methodology. It is not a rigid set of instructions but rather a flexible guide that can be used to build a service management facility that is fit for purpose. Because it is a framework, we should not have to include all of the components. Instead, the key to delivering a service management facility that is fit for purpose is to select the correct components and install them with careful planning. An ITIL Lite project involves selecting those components that work for you and tailoring them accordingly.

1.1 REASONS WHY ITIL MAY NOT BE FULLY IMPLEMENTED

We are so familiar with the reasons *why* we need to implement ITIL that we tend to forget there are also a few reasons why we may *not* want to fully implement it. (Don't forget that there is a difference between reasons and excuses!) For every reason, there is an ITIL Lite approach:

■ **Cost – *the argument*** This is a very common reason and often with justification – especially in light of the change in the financial market in late 2008. Many companies are now looking to cut costs and do not have the budget or resources for full ITIL implementation. In fact, in many cases, it would be quite foolhardy to approach senior management for permission to start a full implementation project.

Cost – *the approach* If cost is a deterrent to full ITIL implementation, then you could start with a Lite version of ITIL as a precursor to full implementation (which could be carried out once the budget is available). Consider a Lite project as phase one and readdress the rest of ITIL when you have completed this phase. Carefully document any savings and successes you may make, and use this data as justification to continue to full implementation.

■ **No customer support – *the argument*** Customer satisfaction is at the heart of service management and a key driving factor for ITIL. However, it is difficult to fully implement ITIL if the customer refuses to cooperate. For example, what is the point in producing service level agreements (SLAs) if the customer will not participate in creating them, or even read them? (This should not stop you producing service targets based on typical SLA contents, though, and then measuring those targets as though you did have SLAs in place.)

No customer support – *the approach* Firstly, you need to determine why the customer does not wish to participate in IT service management activities. Is it because they don't have the time, the inclination or feel the responsibility to do so? Once you have established the cause, with better customer consultation and some ITIL overview education, you can work towards a solution. If you are unable to resolve the problem you can still begin implementation – but start with a Lite version so you don't waste time implementing components that will be ignored. Again, it is

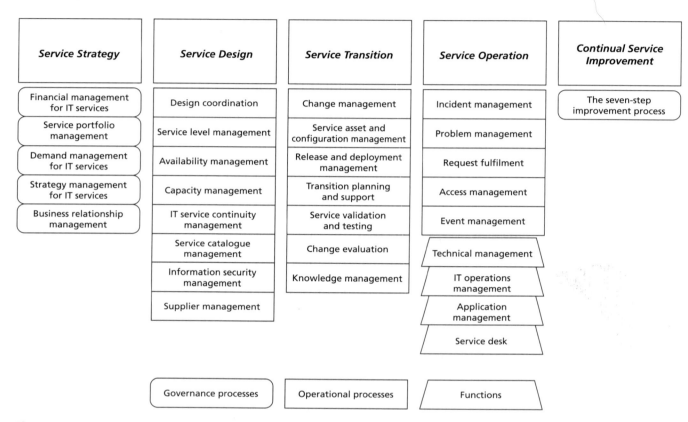

Figure 1.1 ITIL processes and functions

worthwhile to carefully document all of your savings and successes and then use this data as justification to continue to full implementation.

■ **ISO/IEC 20000 limitations – *the argument*** ISO/IEC 20000 was originally designed when ITIL v2 was in place, so many organizations obtained their ISO/IEC 20000 certification by implementing ITIL v2. Since then ISO/IEC 20000 has been updated and is more closely aligned to the service lifecycle. ISO/IEC 20000:1 was updated in 2011, and part 2 in 2012.

ISO/IEC 20000 limitations – *the approach* If your objective is to obtain ISO/IEC 20000 certification, then you do not need to fully implement ITIL. However, ISO/IEC 20000 and ITIL are now more aligned than ever before and, if you value your customers and IT service management enough to obtain ISO/IEC 20000 certification, then you will want to take that extra step. Because full implementation is not necessary for ISO/IEC 20000 certification, ITIL Lite is an ideal solution. A good approach would be to build an ITIL Lite project to help you obtain ISO/IEC 20000 certification, and then progress towards implementing the rest of ITIL.

- **Time constraints – *the argument*** There is no doubt that implementing ITIL is a long and time-consuming project. (After all, one of the reasons that many organizations don't have SLAs in place is because they can't find the time to write them.) Service management is often seen as an operational function and, as such, headcount is just sufficient to support operational activities, leaving no time to implement ITIL.

  Time constraints – *the approach* This is a difficult argument. Assuming additional headcount cannot be created, better use must be made of the existing headcount. In this situation, a full implementation of ITIL is unrealistic. However, you could build an ITIL Lite project that is aimed at releasing staff as part of the plan – for example, staff could be released from the service desk by using problem management to reduce the number of incidents arriving at the service desk, or by implementing change management to keep down the volume of new incidents. In the future, this additional headcount could be used as a development and planning resource.

- **Ownership – *the argument*** It is often assumed that all the components in ITIL are owned by service management whereas, in reality, many of them are owned by other IT departments – for example, you may already have a capacity planning department, an IT service continuity team, or an asset management group. If this is the case, and they report through a different management hierarchy, then it can be very difficult to convince them to participate in your project. While you may be concerned with ITIL configuration, the asset administrator, for example, may have another best practice and as a result be unwilling to participate in an ITIL project that will not benefit asset management.

  Ownership – *the approach* It can be difficult to involve staff from other IT units in an ITIL project, especially if they will not benefit very much from the end result. If they do get involved, they can be too protective and doom the project to failure. Once you have educated them on how they, and the customer, can benefit from ITIL, create and implement an ITIL Lite project that concentrates on those components owned by service management.

- **Running out of steam – *the argument*** This is not really a problem when planning, but does tend to occur during the implementation stage. The enthusiasm which characterizes the beginning of an ITIL project begins to wane, and can be exacerbated by picking the low-hanging fruit first (also known as quick wins). An ITIL implementation project is not like the majority of IT projects that work towards a crescendo. The development of a new service starts with an idea then progresses and grows until the excitement of the day when the new live service is installed. ITIL implementation, on the other hand, starts with energy and enthusiasm but, with no exciting end product, fails to inspire those working on it.

  Running out of steam – *the approach* Set critical success factors and key performance indicators that motivate staff, and reduce the timeframe by removing any ITIL components that will not be implemented from the outset – this way it will not seem like such an endless task.

- **Too complex – *the argument*** This is a common problem because service management staff are practical and familiar with operational activities, but have little or no experience of project design or project management. These skills need to be learnt or imported into service management because being faced with ITIL is a daunting task for the experienced project manager, let alone inexperienced staff.

Too complex – *the approach* Implementing ITIL is a major project and ideally requires an experienced project leader or manager. If such a person is not available then an ITIL Lite project, which concentrates on implementing those components that you are familiar with and confident handling, is an ideal solution. This is a project built around local knowledge and experience, and will ensure service improvement.

■ **V2 already implemented – *the argument*** This is a common argument. Organizations that implemented ITIL v2 may be reluctant to move to a lifecycle-based service management offering. It can be tricky convincing an organization to move to the service lifecycle approach when they are happy with the v2 already in place.

V2 already implemented – *the approach* This is only really valid if all seven v2 publications were consulted and used in the implementation of ITIL v2. Nevertheless, many organizations that followed only *Service Support* and *Service Delivery* are very happy with their service management facility. In this case, the best approach is to compare the current v2 processes and functions with the current ITIL ones and perform a gap analysis to identify the advantages of upgrading. At the same time, review other ITIL components for addition (request fulfilment and event management are popular). The results of this review and the gap analysis will form the basis of your ITIL Lite project.

There are many valid reasons why it may be difficult, or even impossible, for some organizations to fully implement ITIL. However, as you can now see, this should not stop them adopting a critical subset of the components as part of an ITIL Lite initiative.

1.2 LINEAR VERSUS LIFECYCLE APPROACH

In order to understand how a Lite project can fit into the ITIL framework, it is useful to understand the differences and similarities between the linear approach (advocated by ITIL v2) and a lifecycle approach (see Table 1.1).

The ITIL lifecycle approach is most current and it is successful, but v2 does have some merits. The decision over which approach to use – lifecycle or linear – should be a pragmatic one, driven by specific business circumstances and not a judgment about either approach.

ITIL v2 was a framework approach, where implementers were encouraged to build a set of services rather than a service lifecycle. However, one of the problems with this approach was that it concentrated on just two of the core ITIL publications – *Service Support* and *Service Delivery*. As a result, many of those implementing ITIL v2 had never read the other five publications (*Business Perspective*, *Security Management*, *ICT Infrastructure Management*, *Application Management* and *Planning to Implement Service Management*). It does seem odd that those implementing v2 did not actually read *Planning to Implement Service Management*. Only a minority of organizations that undertook v2 achieved full implementation – although those that did achieve partial implementation improved their services.

Table 1.1 Linear versus lifecycle approach

Linear approach (v2)	Lifecycle approach
Concentrated on the essentials	Takes a lifecycle approach
Is static	Is organic
Built around a much smaller ITSM role	Sees ITSM as a major IT function
Developed from a small contribution pool	Developed from a large international pool
Pick and choose – did anyone read all seven publications?	You have to read all of the publications

V2 tended to focus on the essentials rather than the broader picture of service management. The lifecycle approach, on the other hand, encourages users to look at the lifecycle of services, not just key components, while ITIL qualifications and certification are aimed at all of the publications. The lifecycle approach may seem like a more daunting task – but not if you consider the five ignored v2 publications.

The ITIL 2011 editions are the latest, and recommended, guidance on ITIL. They are a good solution and will provide the foundations of any new iterations that may appear in the future. It is possible, however, to build an ITIL Lite solution around the v2 *Service Support* and *Service Delivery* components if they are already in existence (see sections 5.1.3 and 5.1.4).

1.3 WHY YOU CANNOT IMPLEMENT THE ITIL SERVICE LIFECYCLE USING A LINEAR APPROACH

For most people, implementing ITIL v2 was made easy by its framework approach, which allowed you to implement the components in a random manner (because it was a framework; see Figure 1.2).

A typical ITIL v2 project began by implementing *Service Support* and this is where many implementations ended. Those that did not end at this point continued on to *Service Delivery*. All of the components in *Service Support* were operational-style activities and compare closely with *ITIL Service Operation* and *ITIL Service Transition* (which are both predominately operational).

Most of the components in v2 *Service Support* were already being performed, to some degree, in many IT organizations – with the exception of configuration management. Therefore, to implement v2 *Service Support*, organizations conducted a simple gap analysis between current operations and the ITIL v2 recommendations, and made the necessary changes.

The *Service Support* components were logical processes but the *Service Delivery* components were more complicated management functions. Not all of the components in v2 *Service Delivery* were already in operation to the same degree as the v2 *Service Support* components. For example, in many organizations, capacity management was ad hoc or on demand rather than a clearly defined activity.

Implementing the ITIL service lifecycle is a very different challenge. The lifecycle approach is aimed at managing the lifecycle of a service, and therefore

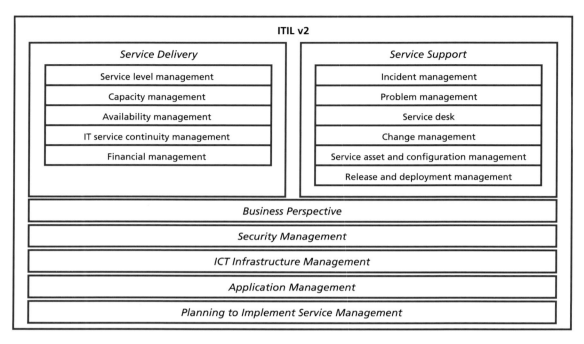

Figure 1.2 ITIL v2 framework

components do not need to be implemented in a particular order. This means that it is not necessary to start at page 1 of *ITIL Service Strategy* and progress through the publications until you reach the last page of *ITIL Continual Service Improvement*.

The lifecycle approach can be illustrated with some examples: availability and capacity need to know the configuration of a service if they are to provide proper service management support, but they are in the *ITIL Service Design* publication, which comes before *ITIL Service Transition* where service asset and configuration management resides. Similarly, change management can affect just about every component but it is in *ITIL Service Transition*, which is the third publication in the lifecycle. If incident and change management were poor, surely you would work on these first?

None of the processes in ITIL has the word 'process' as part of its name. This is because most of the components are much more than just a process. For example, within capacity management there is a capacity measuring process, but a capacity planning function would also be required – another reason why implementing ITIL can sometimes be so difficult.

To fully understand the linear (v2) and lifecycle comparison, and see how the two approaches fit together, it is useful to overlay the v2 *Service Support* and *Service Delivery* publications onto the ITIL 2011 publications. Figure 1.3 shows how the *Service Support* components fit into the operational publications – the very heart of IT service management.

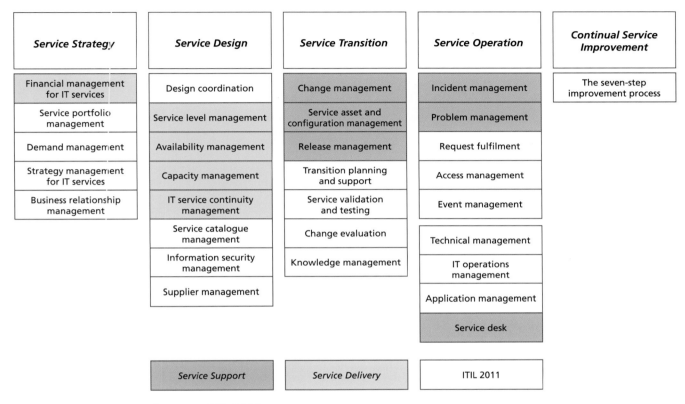

Service Strategy	Service Design	Service Transition	Service Operation	Continual Service Improvement
Financial management for IT services	Design coordination	Change management	Incident management	The seven-step improvement process
Service portfolio management	Service level management	Service asset and configuration management	Problem management	
Demand management	Availability management	Release management	Request fulfilment	
Strategy management for IT services	Capacity management	Transition planning and support	Access management	
Business relationship management	IT service continuity management	Service validation and testing	Event management	
	Service catalogue management	Change evaluation	Technical management	
	Information security management	Knowledge management	IT operations management	
	Supplier management		Application management	
			Service desk	

Service Support	Service Delivery	ITIL 2011

Figure 1.3 ITIL v2 overlay onto ITIL 2011

Imagine ITIL 2011 as a ship, where *ITIL Service Strategy* and *ITIL Service Design* are navigators, and *ITIL Service Transition* and *ITIL Service Operation* are the engine room – without an engine, navigation won't get you anywhere. But, with an engine and minimal navigation tools, you can get almost anywhere. The ITIL service lifecycle is here to stay, even if we can only adopt a Lite version.

1.4 SUMMARY

ITIL is a framework, not a methodology and, as such, it can be tailored to an organization's individual needs. The key phrase to remember is 'fit for purpose'. ITIL is now based on a lifecycle approach which is why any implementation – full or partial – cannot be linear. Now we understand the philosophy behind ITIL we can begin to look towards building an implementation project and, if full implementation is not a possibility, then ITIL Lite is an ideal solution. The first step in our ITIL Lite project is to establish a systematic approach to process engineering.

A simple but effective approach to ITIL process engineering

2

2 A simple but effective approach to ITIL process engineering

Each component should be implemented to the highest quality in an ITIL Lite project, and this is why we need a simple but effective approach to ITIL process engineering. There are some excellent process engineering practices that you can follow (Six Sigma™, for example) but, in a Lite scenario, it is probable that the project will not have the people or financial resources available to become proficient in a process engineering best practice. For this reason, you may have to perform your own process engineering.

2.1 WHY YOU NEED A SYSTEMATIC APPROACH TO PROCESS ENGINEERING

It is possible that different people will work on building different ITIL Lite components at the same time, which is why clear project guidance is essential if the final result is to be consistent. A systematic approach is a standardized way of working. It ensures consistency and standard terminology, and means that all project teams will produce processes that have the same look, feel and vocabulary. The advantages of adopting a systematic approach include:

■ **A consistent look and feel** We usually associate this with screen displays and icons but the same principle can also be applied to process design and documentation. A consistent look and feel

promotes familiarity which, in turn, allows users to become comfortable with the construction of processes and follow them logically.

■ **Ongoing learning** This is one of the most natural ways to learn. Process creation is like any other tool – the more you use it, the better you get at using it. If you have a systematic approach in place for creating processes, then this in itself becomes your practice and, as you build more processes, your skills will improve to the benefit of your processes.

■ **Faster development of processes** As knowledge increases, as a result of ongoing learning, so the development of future processes will accelerate.

■ **Clear metrics** To ensure successful process design, incorporate both performance and quality metrics. A well-designed systematic approach should contain guidelines to include these metrics and eliminate any guesswork.

■ **A process that is easy to teach and learn** Like any other activity, process development is a skill that can be learnt. Not all ITIL Lite project teams will include a specialist project engineer, which means that service management may have to develop the processes itself – with little or no previous process engineering experience. It is also likely that the owners of the various ITIL components will be involved in building their own processes (for example, the service desk manager may be involved in developing the incident management process). A systematic approach makes it easier to teach inexperienced process developers how to develop a process.

■ **Credibility** As staff, peers, customers and management see processes being successfully developed, so the credibility of both the processes and service management will increase. This credibility will often encourage support and, in some circumstances, perhaps funding. A fragmented approach, in which every participant creates their own unique process, will not achieve the same credibility.

■ **A project that is easy to manage** With the development of multiple processes, it is far easier for a project leader to monitor the progress of the project if each process follows a consistent approach and is developed using the same ground rules.

Developing processes doesn't have to be expensive. Most processes are logical – obvious even – when fancy words and techniques are stripped away.

2.2 WHY THE PROCESSES MUST INCORPORATE MORE THAN ITIL

The world of IT is much greater than ITIL and, therefore, our Lite project must incorporate more than ITIL. Firstly, we need to take into account governance, which is both a friend and a foe. On a positive note, Sarbanes-Oxley helped many organizations raise the revenues for asset and configuration resources that otherwise would not have been provided. On the other hand, even though governance is essential it can be frustrating when, for example, it limits our ability to build useful information resources – such as a data protection regulation that stops us storing sensitive data in our files.

Governance has gained prominence over the last few years with the introduction of regulations figure-headed by Sarbanes-Oxley. There are essentially four forms of governance which we need to consider when building our ITIL Lite project:

■ **Regulatory (national/international) governance** This is the highest level of governance, usually backed up by punitive legislation, typically Sarbanes-Oxley and data protection Acts. We have no choice but to follow this level of governance, and we will be audited to check that we are complying. We must be careful as we build our ITIL Lite project that we adhere to this level of governance.

■ **Industry governance** This may not have the muscle of the previous level of governance but it can still pack a knockout punch. It concerns those regulations that relate to the business sector in which your organization operates – for example, BASEL II for banking or HIPPA for the health sector. Although not as punitive as regulatory governance, it still has to be obeyed. If you have industry governance you will almost certainly be aware of it but, if you are in any doubt, check.

■ **Company governance** Many organizations around the world have their own code of practice, which they expect their staff and associates to follow. Obviously, the punishment for breaking company regulations is not as severe as it is for the higher levels of governance, but people have been sacked for not adhering to them. Where they exist, you should be aware of them.

■ **Departmental governance** Often known as IT standards, this level of governance places rules and policies on various IT activities. If these codes exist, staff members must be familiar with them.

These four forms of governance have one thing in common – they all provide constraints to ensure that IT does not abuse its position within an organization.

As well as governance, an ITIL implementation project must also take into account best practices (which are slightly different from governance). A best practice is:

> 'A method or technique that has consistently shown results superior to those achieved with other means, and that is used as a benchmark.' (**www.businessdictionary.com/definition/best-practice.html**)

Any implementation project must incorporate both governance and best practice. With governance as the foundation stone, we can begin to build a best-practices structure:

- **Foundation stone – governance** It makes sense that the fundamental rules that we have to adhere to form the basis of an ITIL Lite project.
- **Service management layer – ITIL and business process models** On top of the foundation stone we can put ITIL and the business process models. You could argue that the key role of service management is to support the business processes; therefore they can appear on the same level.
- **Controls layer – COBIT** ITIL provides great guidance for building operational processes and procedures, but it does not offer much advice on managing quality and accuracy. This is where COBIT® (Control OBjectives for Information and related Technology) comes in. In simple terms, COBIT is a practice that applies checks and balances to IT and, in particular, service management processes.

- **Process engineering layer – Six Sigma** By utilizing ITIL, we can make sure that our processes will be both accurate and of a high quality, but how do you build quality processes? Six Sigma is an appropriate IT process-building methodology with the fundamental objective of reducing errors. However, in an ITIL Lite project it may not be possible to adopt Six Sigma and, as a result, organizations may undertake their own process engineering (see section 2.3).
- **Process maturity layer – CMMI** Once built, we need to know that our processes are working and maturing successfully. This requires another layer in the structure. Capability Maturity Model Integration (CMMI) takes an existing process to another level by establishing target levels of maturity. It uses a hierarchy of five levels (where each level is described as a level of maturity).
- **Overall objective – ISO/IEC 20000** CMMI could be the final building block in our pyramid, but perhaps we should ask ourselves why we are embarking on this ITIL Lite project – what is our mission and the ultimate deliverable? Well, ISO/IEC 20000 would certainly be a candidate. ISO/IEC 20000 certification may not be the mission of the project, but it is a great benchmark to aim for. We now have the complete picture (see Figure 2.1): our governance layer, our service management layer, our controls layer, our process engineering layer, our processes maturity layer and, at the top of the pyramid, our overall objective.

It is essential that any project takes into consideration governance and supporting best practices. These best practices have been chosen because they are fit for purpose, they figure in the ITIL publications, and they are geared to work with ITIL.

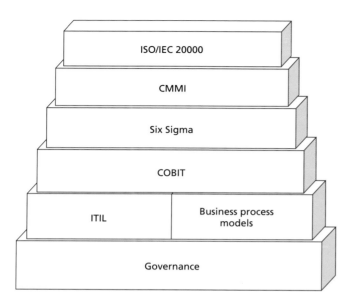

Figure 2.1 Best-practices pyramid

2.3 PROCESS DESIGN FOR ITIL LITE

Although the Six Sigma approach to process design and process improvement is ideal, many organizations lack the funds or time to adopt it and, as a result, require some guidance on building processes. Many of the ITIL processes are iterative and, as such, fairly easy to identify – for example, in many organizations, incident management was already being performed well by the service desk before ITIL was introduced. Developing and creating processes can include just two steps:

- **Step 1** Design the process flow
- **Step 2** Document the flow (this would also include installing metrics, etc.).

This may sound oversimplified but, as we will see, it is in fact quite logical.

There are two basic process-flow elements (see Figure 2.2):

- **Transmission** The method to get from one process activity to another process activity – for example, an email may be sent from the service desk to second-level support to escalate an incident; the transmission is an email. Similarly, if a text message was sent, then that would be the transmission method. Performance savings can often be gained by improving transmission methods. A good example of this is the savings made by replacing escalation telephone calls with automated escalation using incident management technology. Sometimes, if one person is performing a number of consecutive activities, the transmission methods between those activities would be described as 'at source'.
- **Activity** Where an activity has to be performed as a stage or step in the process. For example, some incident management activities include incident escalation, allocating a priority and incident closure. Activities can be manual or automated.

Figure 2.3 is part of an example incident process:

- Transmission arrives from a previous activity. In this case, the transmission was performed by the incident management tool 'at source', which means that it involved one person using the incident management tool to perform the actual transmission.
- Next is the incident escalation activity, where the incident is analysed to decide on the recipient of the escalated incident.
- Once the activity has been determined, the next step is to email the incident to the recipient. Email is the transmission method.
- When the incident arrives at source it has to be reviewed by the recipient.

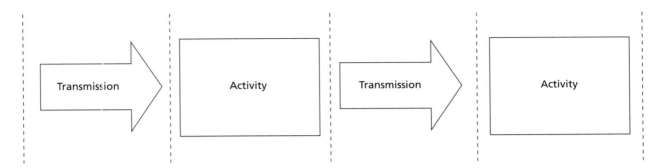

Figure 2.2 Process transmission and activity components

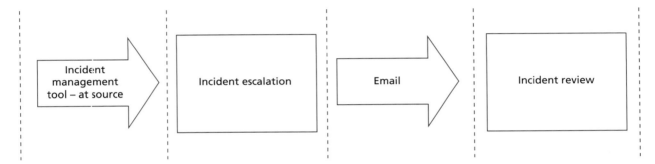

Figure 2.3 Example of process transmission and activity actions

Although we can build solid processes from the two elements (transmissions and activities), they only show us the flow and do not explain how we should perform our activities. That's the job of a work instruction.

Work instructions are often procedure-based and explain how we should perform our activities. They are also used to build the parameters and rules for automation technology. For example, you would use an existing work instruction to enter priority levels and rules into an incident management tool. Work instructions are linked to the action, but they are not related to the transmissions (see Figure 2.4).

Each activity should, ideally, have a work instruction. The work instructions provide information about how an activity should be performed (see Figure 2.5). This information can then be used in the automation of work instructions and activities.

The 'procedure on how to escalate an incident' would include when to escalate, who to escalate to, and how to escalate so that the person escalating the incident knows exactly how to perform the activities. Likewise, the 'incident review instructions' would explain exactly what needs to be reviewed by the recipient and the action to take if the incident has been wrongly escalated.

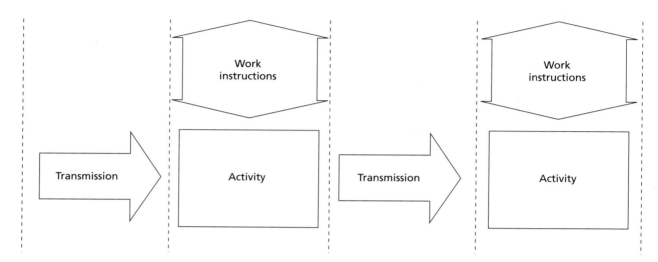

Figure 2.4 Work instruction components

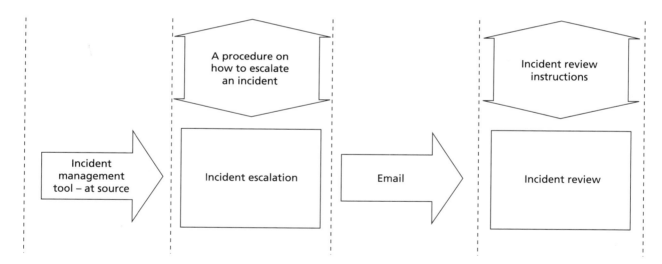

Figure 2.5 Work instruction example

In a process, the elements (activity, transmission and work instructions) stay static in the same sequence. However, the actions required to process these elements can vary – for example, in Figure 2.5 the transmission method is an email, but it could easily be a telephone call or a text message. The processes remain in the same location no matter how many different transmission methods are available.

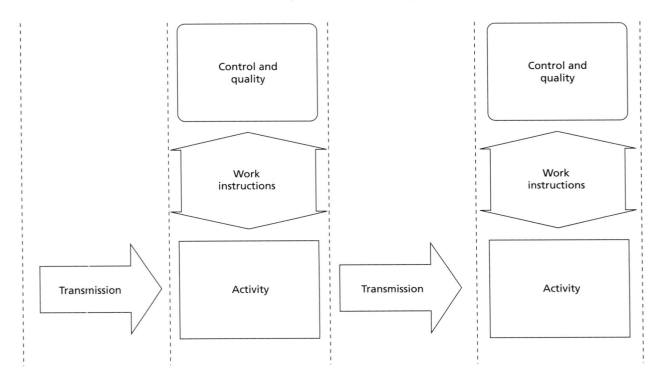

Figure 2.6 Control and quality element

Control and quality is the final piece in the jigsaw, where we put in place rules, controls and metrics to ensure the highest possible levels of quality and accuracy (see Figure 2.6).

Figure 2.6 shows how control and quality fits in to the overall scope of a successful process. It also shows how important work instructions are to process operation, because they link an activity to control and quality.

Figure 2.7 shows how the whole thing fits together. The control and quality element is pressuring the activities to meet clear levels of quality and accuracy.

What we have described so far is an approach to building self-contained processes. However, an activity in one process will often trigger the start of another process, or link into an activity in another process (see Figure 2.8).

The linkage in Figure 2.8 is a bi-directional arrow. This is because an activity in one process can link to another process and stimulate that process into action or, in turn, be stimulated itself by an activity in another process. Figure 2.9 shows an example of this.

The work instruction element in Figure 2.9 states that 'if a Priority 1 is allocated then the business contingency process must be initiated'. This

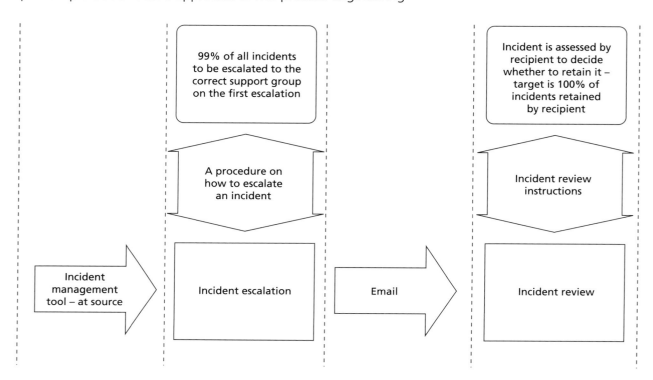

Figure 2.7 Control and quality example

means that, as the illustration shows, the incident escalation activity now has two functions – one is to email the incident to a support group and the other is to initiate the business contingency process. Linkage is a crucial element because you have to decide whether to have one large process, with several forks, or a number of discrete processes that can be linked as required.

A discrete process is a stand-alone process that can be completed in a linear fashion without impact from another process (the incident management process is a discrete process). The exception is when a link is included to another discrete process – for

example, problem management is a discrete process that will require a link to change management so that a root cause can be eliminated.

An incident management process may have a number of potential linkages, including links to problem management, business contingency, change management, configuration management and event management.

Looking at Figure 2.10, part (a), it is easy to see how quickly a compound map of processes can become complicated. Part (b), on the other hand, is much easier to understand.

Part (a) illustrates the following scenario:

- An incident has arrived at the service desk, step C1
- This incident cannot be resolved and therefore has to be passed to problem management, from step C2 to B1
- Problem management has found the solution but needs to go to change management for authorization, step B2 to A4
- The incident has been resolved in change management, step A5 to A6

- Change management notifies problem management, step A7 to B5
- Problem management updates and closes the record, and informs incident management, step B5 to C6
- Incident management then completes the final activities – customer notification and record closure – step C7 to C8.

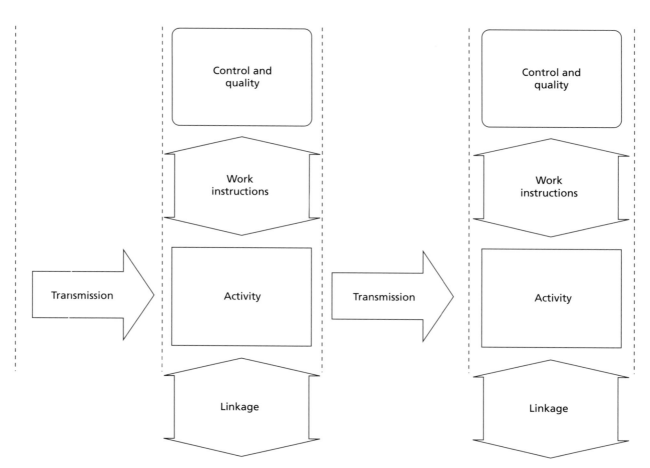

Figure 2.8 Process linkage

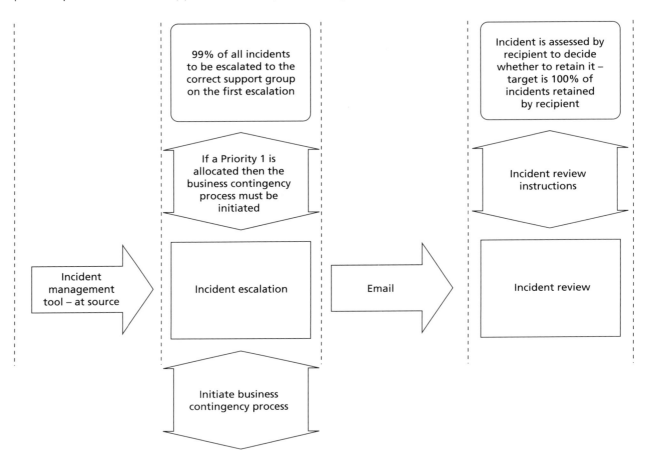

Figure 2.9 Example of a linkage element

Any steps missed out here would have been completed within their processes (this is just an example, processes haven't been described in detail). On average, over 90% of incidents are resolved without involving change management so why create a complex compound process map to include every link to change management? It makes more sense to have linkages built into the processes as shown in part (b).

As services and technologies change, IT will continue to morph and, in turn, processes will evolve. This is why ITSM processes need to be flexible and not part of a compound process map. The processes shown in part (b) would have linkages built in which can be easily changed and updated as required. Discrete processes reduce process development time and improve flexibility. Discrete processes are:

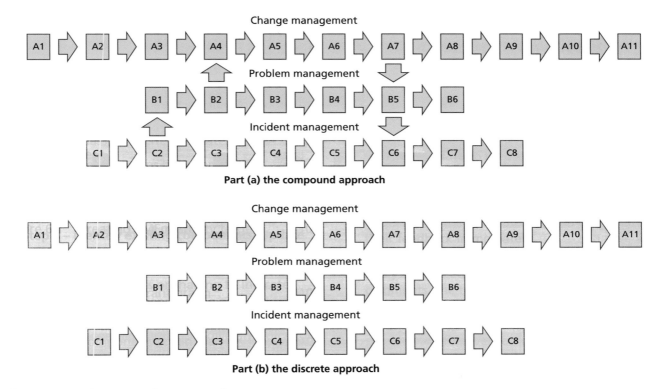

Figure 2.10 Discrete and compound process maps

- **Locally managed** Each of the discrete processes can be managed locally – for example, the service desk could manage the incident process. This ensures that the process owners are responsible for following the processes, which gives them a greater stake in their own decisions and efficiency. Staff perform better when they own, rather than just use, a process.
- **Locally maintained** If the processes are to be managed locally then it makes sense to have them maintained locally too. However, you should ensure that any changes are reported through the change management process.

- **Flexible** Discrete processes are more flexible because they allow for anomalies to be handled quickly and then addressed as required. For example, a missed linkage element could be actioned and then formally documented later. This reduces downtime for customers and allows staff the flexibility to make key decisions without having to blindly follow rigid processes.

It is often difficult to decide which processes are discrete and which should have branches. In the case of ITIL, this is relatively straightforward because each of the 26 governance and operational processes identified in Figure 1.1 qualifies as a discrete process.

2.4 MONITORING ITIL PROCESSES

In section 2.2 we looked at best practices including COBIT, which is closely linked to ITIL. Keep COBIT and other best practices in mind because quality, as well as performance, needs to be measured. Control and quality was one of the basic process elements (see Figure 2.8).

Figure 2.11 shows that ITIL drives the flow of the processes and COBIT drives the control and quality element of the processes. We must keep this in mind as we design our ITIL Lite processes. As a general rule, for every activity there should be elements for work instructions, and control and quality. There will, of course, be exceptions but consider the rule carefully before breaking it.

The work instructions and control and quality elements give us a standard approach for the implementation and a basis for the metrics required to measure both the performance and quality of our ITIL Lite processes. The key to a successful process is how accurately each activity can be performed, and then how quickly the activity or transmission can be performed to meet those levels.

Figure 2.12 shows how performance can be measured. The transmission and activity timings tell us how long it takes to perform each step. These are usually fairly easy to monitor, especially when they are performed electronically or measured in a tool.

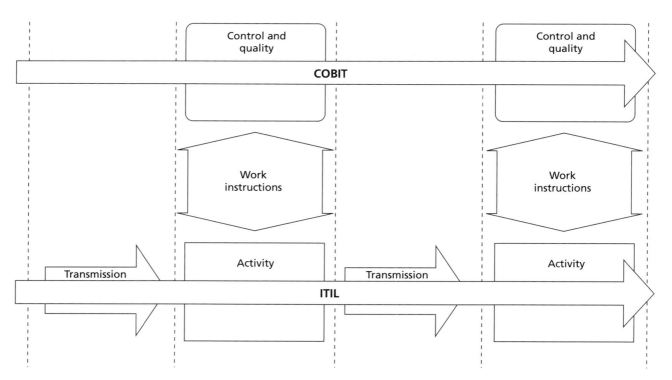

Figure 2.11 ITIL, COBIT and the process elements

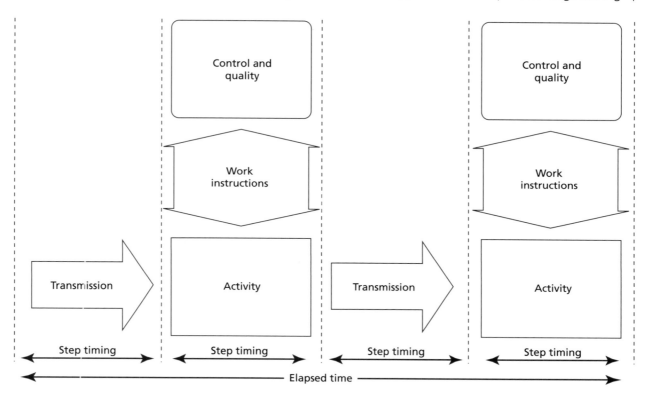

Figure 2.12 Process performance measurement points

An incident management tool, for example, will record when an incident arrives at the service desk and then each activity as it happens.

Quality is not as easy to measure because, in some cases, it will require integrity and honesty on behalf of the process operatives. Problems can be encountered when, for example, the target for successfully closed incidents is 99% and a service desk agent, instead of reopening an incident, opens a new incident. This would mean that the original incident would register as a successfully closed incident. Process operatives must be trained and understand the need to perform their duties diligently because this data helps processes to evolve and aids operatives in the execution of their duties.

The process metrics example in Figure 2.13 contains both performance and quality metrics. Let's look at the performance metrics first. As Figure 2.13 illustrates, each step has a target metric and an actual metric, so it's easy to monitor relative performance. In the first step of Figure 2.13, why was the actual average 5 seconds against a target of 10 seconds? Was it due to a change in the transmission technology, or just an exceptional period (for example, a drop in business demand of the service)? If we look just at the overall metrics we

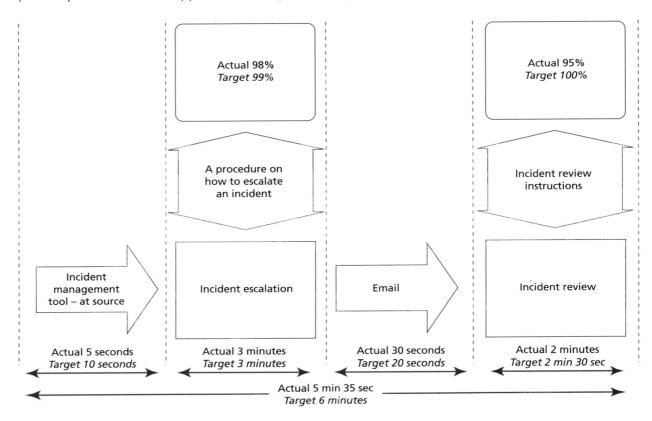

Figure 2.13 Process metrics example

can see that the actual was 25 seconds faster than the target but, when we look at the step metrics, we can see how this was achieved (and identify those elements that were underperforming). These figures are an example of a given period (monthly) but you can divide them as you wish.

The quality metrics add context to the performance metrics. The actual performance of incident escalation was the same as its target, but the quality was lower than its target. Incident review is performing at an impressive 30 seconds faster than the set target but is underperforming against the quality target – this would indicate that more time should be spent on getting it right.

Monitoring performance is a delicate balancing act; sometimes you have to sacrifice a little quality for performance, or vice versa. More time can improve quality, but you need to establish whether that time is actually available and if the targets are realistic. Changing one target will have an impact on the other metrics.

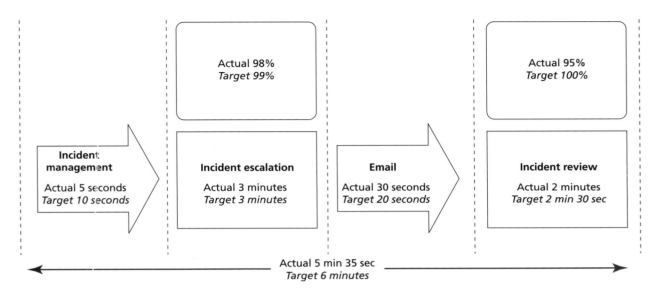

Figure 2.14 Presenting process metrics

When presenting metrics, they will make much more sense if they are shown in the context of the process structure. This makes them easier to understand and continues to endorse the structure of the process to all who read the report. A graphic, similar to Figure 2.14, could be created for a process and each of the elements made into a hyperlink with more detailed data behind the element, which would inform without confusing.

2.5   BUILDING ITIL LITE PROCESSES

Building processes can be daunting, even for an experienced process engineer. However, if you have a systematic approach in place, a potentially stressful experience can become an interesting and enjoyable one. The best way to approach process building is to have a clear procedure in place.

Figure 2.15 outlines the procedure for building ITIL Lite processes. There are 22 steps:

■ **Identify a discrete process** You may want to select a process that you already have in place (e.g. incident management) as a basis for developing a discrete process.

■ **Write a goal for the discrete process** Because ITIL Lite is based on the latest ITIL guidance, the process objectives should reflect the objectives as they are defined in the publications. For example, if we were looking to build a change management process, then the *ITIL Service Transition* publication outlines the purpose and objectives of change management, and the purpose and objectives of the change management process.

If you are creating ITIL processes then it is your job to deliver the objectives as they are described in the relevant publication. Additions to the ITIL description may, of course, be made but do not remove any data without careful consideration.

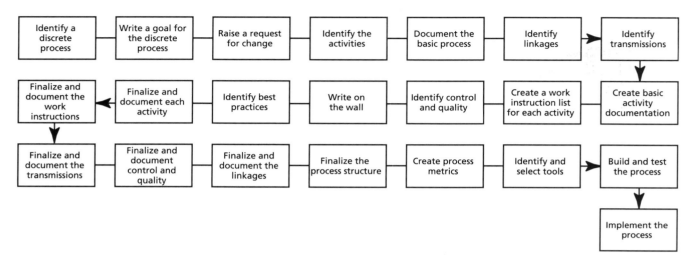

Figure 2.15 Procedure for building a process

If you feel that you cannot use the ITIL process objectives then you will need to create your own at this point.

■ **Raise a request for change** In order to follow the recommended ITIL procedure a request for change (RFC), which includes the goals of the project, should be raised. If you do not have a method for submitting an RFC, an RFC is not required, or there's no formal change management then the goals of the project should be distributed to all interested parties and their feedback obtained.

Once your RFC has been approved, or you have reached a consensus on the objectives, you are ready to continue. Because ITIL change management will not have yet been implemented, you will have to use the current change management system.

■ **Identify the activities** Mistakes at this point can cause considerable problems later on. Involve all those who use and understand the current process, and make sure you have the appropriate ITIL publication to hand. Some of the ITIL processes are so well documented in the publications that most of the work has already been done for you.

For example, Figure 2.16, adapted from *ITIL Service Operation,* gives a clear outline of the problem management process. It is a good example of a discrete process, with linkage to change management.

The processes for event, incident, change and evaluation management are also well documented in the ITIL publications. Unless you have significant problems with these published processes, you should use them when implementing your ITIL Lite project.

For all other processes, use the publication as a guide and produce your own process. To identify the activities for a process, keep asking yourself 'What comes next?' (There are five questions that we will need to consider over the next five steps; see Figure 2.17). The process steps flow logically

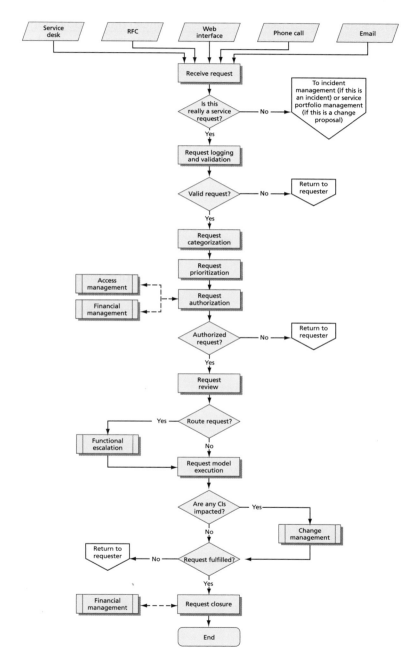

Figure 2.16 ITIL problem management process (from **ITIL Service Operation)**

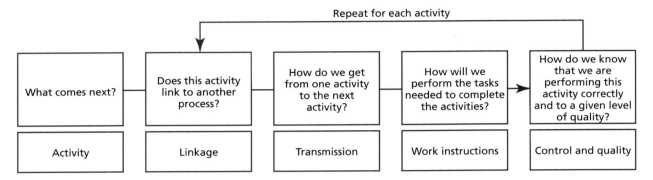

Figure 2.17 The five key process questions

in Figure 2.16, with each providing an answer to this question. If there are two answers to this question then you will need a linkage point.

When identifying a later step, it often becomes obvious that an earlier step has been missed, and the process will need to be updated (this is why it is so important to have in place a system that is easy to update).

You can use a specialist software tool specifically designed to engineer processes, although this can be expensive, and difficult to learn unless you have a process engineer in the team. You could also use tools that are not specifically built for process design but can be used to draw process diagrams (e.g. Microsoft PowerPoint). Another effective, albeit simple, method is sticky notes:

- Decide on the first activity in the process
- Write the name of that activity on a sticky note and place it on the wall
- Repeat for all activities in the process
- Arrange the sticky notes until you are confident that you have all the activities in the correct order

- Invite some people who are close to the process for their opinion and make changes to your processes where it makes sense to do so
- When you are confident, number and collect your sticky notes
- You can now draw your process chart, using a product such as Microsoft Word or Microsoft PowerPoint if you do not have a specialized tool, and taking Figure 2.16 as an example.

This is an effective method which allows three or four people to contribute at the same time. (We will see more of this method later, in 'Write on the wall'.)

- **Document the basic process** Now the activities are in order, you need to write a small description for each one. These descriptions should be circulated to anyone who was involved in the previous step, inviting them to give feedback. It is a good idea, at this point, to create a documentation system to centrally store all of the information. This can easily be done electronically.
- **Identify linkages** We have already asked the question 'What comes next?'; now we need to ask 'Does this activity link to another process?'

Make a note in the documentation system when an activity links to another process, or processes, ensuring that the reason for the linkage is also described.

■ **Identify transmissions** With the activities in place, we have to decide the transmission method for each activity – 'How do we get from one activity to the next activity?' Do not be selective at this point if there is more than one transmission method, or even potentially more than one. List them here, so that all possibilities can be explored (the list of possibilities can be finalized later). Don't forget that, as you identify each transmission method, you should document it in your documentation system.

■ **Create basic activity documentation** Basic activity documentation should describe the functions that are to be performed by the activities – if the activity was to decide which priority is to be allocated, then this should be clearly explained so that the work instructions and quality elements can be created to allocate and measure the priorities.

■ **Create a work instruction list for each activity** The next question to answer is 'How will we perform the tasks needed to complete the activities?' All actions, whether manual or automated, should be listed. When you start to look at the tasks you may realize that you'll have to divide some activities into two separate activities. A bullet list is sufficient, as formal documentation will come later. A bulleted list may help to create any procedures that may be required for control purposes.

■ **Identify control and quality** The final question we need to ask ourselves is 'How do we know that we are performing this activity correctly and to a given level of quality?' The types of controls and quality measures required for premium service need to be identified for each activity. It is not necessary to define precise values here – a description such as 'A high level of incidents must be escalated correctly' would be sufficient – or you could add an approximate value: 'Incidents must be escalated correctly 90–95% of the time'. Remember that, at this stage, we are still engineering the process – we will get into more detail in later steps. We have now answered the five key process questions (see Figure 2.17) and can move on to the next step in the process-building procedure.

■ **Write on the wall** The next stage in building a process is to get as much constructive input as possible. One way to do this is to send copies of all the information in the documentation system to those who will be involved in, or affected by, the process. This can be effective but assumes that people will read the documentation and, due to misunderstandings, can sometimes provide more questions than answers. Another, more interactive, method is 'writing on the wall' where the activities are posted onto the wall of a conference room and all interested parties are invited to add their comments. Figure 2.18 shows what a writing-on-the-wall chart would look like. Write the name of each activity on a separate piece of flipchart paper and divide each of the sheets into five equal parts, labelling each section with the process element and relevant key process question (see Figure 2.17). To give your guests an idea of where this activity sits in the process, indicate its position at the top of the chart. Print out all the documentation to date and attach it to the relevant element before posting the flipcharts to a conference room wall, in sequence.

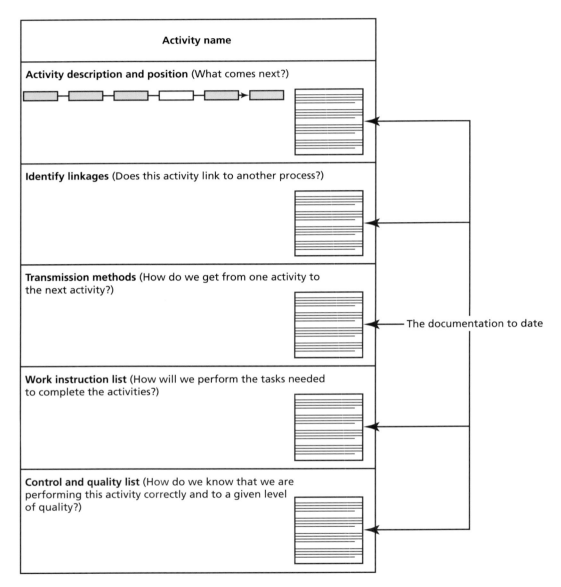

Figure 2.18 Writing-on-the-wall charts

You are now ready to write on the wall:

- Invite your first set of guests – those who will either be affected by, or involved in, the processes.
- Give each guest a pad of sticky notes on which to write their comments. Once they have written their comments they should then stick them on the appropriate activity flipchart, in the correct segment of that chart.
- Encourage your guests to ask questions; ensure that you understand their comments and, if necessary, discuss them further.
- Your guests should walk along the wall until they are happy that they have made a relevant contribution.
- Repeat steps for your next set of guests.
- Work through all of your guests, documenting their comments in the documentation system.

You will now have all the comments and suggestions included in your documentation system. One of the advantages of this approach is that all of the comments and suggestions are stored at the appropriate place in the process, which reduces time when updating the documentation. This can be a fun exercise, and also a productive one because it encourages open discourse and does not require specialized skills. Sometimes 'writing on the wall' can be so popular that it may be wise to schedule an 'open house' session for the curious and forgotten. Be warned, though, that you could become overwhelmed with information. The goals of this step are to verify the process, get ideas to improve it, collate data on all of the elements of the process, engage relevant people in the development of the process and increase the likelihood of its success. Once you have reviewed and updated your process flow, distribute the documentation. Feedback should be reviewed, and adjustments made if necessary.

- **Identify best practices** You have already chosen ITIL; now you need to consider other relevant best practices (see section 2.2). It's strongly recommended that you look closely at COBIT and if you have a governance officer, or someone similar, they will be able to offer help and support during this stage. At the end of this step, you should have identified those best practices which will be adopted, or potentially adopted.
- **Finalize and document each activity** There are three different approaches (see Figure 2.19) that can be used to complete this step and the next four.

This step and the next four steps essentially follow the same pattern (to double-check the elements before finalizing the documentation); it is just the approach that differs. You need to select your preferred approach from the three illustrated in Figure 2.19:

- **Part (a) – the linear approach** In this approach all the steps are completed in a linear order. For example, if there were 12 activities in your process then you would firstly finalize and document all 12 activities, and then finalize and document all 12 sets of work instructions, and so on through the next three elements. This approach has the advantage of concentrating on one element at a time, but it can be easy to lose track of the overall process.
- **Part (b) – the full-loop approach** This approach is essentially the opposite of the linear approach. The first activity is finalized and documented, and then the work instructions for that activity, and then the transmissions etc. So, using our example of

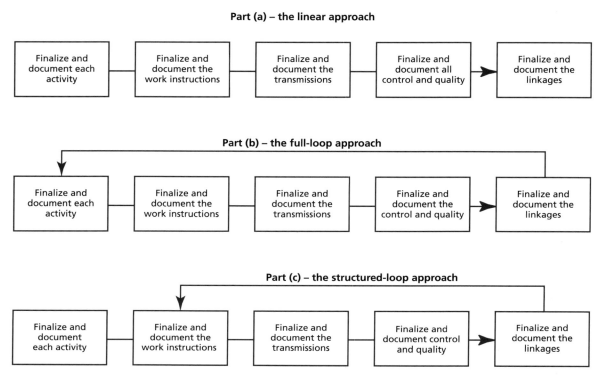

Figure 2.19 Approaches to finalizing and documenting process elements

12 activities, all the elements for each activity are completed before progressing on to the next activity. This approach allows you to concentrate your resources on one activity at a time, ensuring good connectivity between the activity elements.

● **Part (c) – the structured-loop approach** This approach is an amalgam of the previous approaches. It starts by finalizing and documenting all of the activities, and then looping to document the other elements for each component. Using the example of 12 you would first finalize and document all 12 activities and then return to the first

activity and document the other elements for that activity, and so on until all activities are complete.

Once you have chosen your approach you can begin finalizing and documenting your activities. Firstly, the method for storing and presenting the documentation should be chosen. Based on the activities that you have defined, update the process flow diagram that you produced for the approach that you selected, then review your current documentation for accuracy and content. An independent assessor or quality controller should read and check that each activity is easy to understand and fit for purpose. At the end of this step you should have the final draft documentation for your activities ready.

■ **Finalize and document the work instructions** Complete this step according to whichever approach you chose in the previous step. Ensure that the work instructions are tested by the operational team that will be expected to perform them. Remember that the work instructions will also provide the rules and parameters for automated systems, so make sure that they are clear and precise. At the end of this step, the work instructions should be documented and tested.

■ **Finalize and document the transmissions** How you complete this step will depend upon which approach you chose in the 'Finalize and document each activity' step. The performance of a process is often dictated by the transmission methods used to progress from one activity to another. Document how the transmission should happen and what information will be carried in it. Don't start choosing methods or tools at this point – that will be done later.

■ **Finalize and document control and quality** When we identified our control and quality components for each activity we hadn't yet considered best practices. Now, using our chosen approach (linear, full-loop or structured-loop) we can apply these best practices to our process steps, and review control and quality.

■ **Finalize and document the linkages** This is the final step to be completed in the linear, full-loop or structured-loop approach. It has been left until last because it is possible that new linkages may have been identified when completing the previous four steps. Here, in our final documentation, we need to identify each linkage and the conditions that apply to it. Often, the best way to do this is to treat the linkage as an activity and include the other elements (e.g. work instructions, control and quality, and transmission) to get a complete picture.

■ **Finalize the process structure** This is a run-through to check that everything has been documented, and that the process flow works. Any problems with the process should be eliminated at this point. At the end of this stage, the final process flow and all its associated documentation should be ready. This should be circulated for feedback and then published.

■ **Create process metrics** With all of the documentation in place we can now look at what metrics we are going to apply. Metrics are important because they influence training and tool selection. Bear in mind that we need both performance and quality metrics. The best method is to work through the process in sequence, going from activity to transmission, activity to transmission, until metrics have been created for the whole process.

Figure 2.20 shows the points at which we need to look for performance and quality metrics. The overall performance target reflects the target duration of the process from end to end. This is important in areas of high performance (e.g. incident management) but less important for more content-driven processes (e.g. change management). Overall performance is not always relevant but, where it is, it's significant.

Step-by-step metrics are the timings of the activities and transmissions which, when added together, constitute the overall performance metrics. These are very important because by tweaking them the overall performance timing can be reduced. These metrics are also affected by the methods utilized to perform the activities

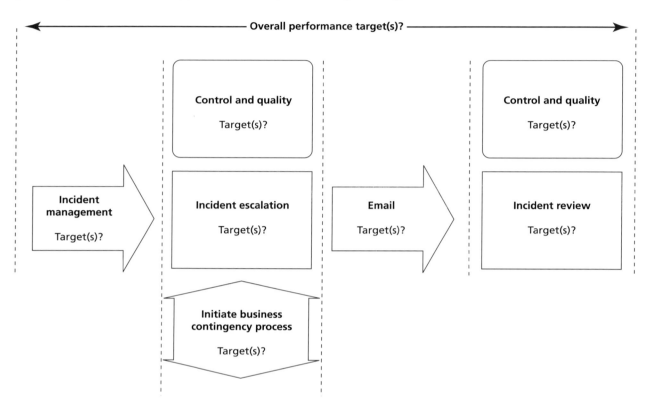

Figure 2.20 Metrics and the process flow

– so, again, savings in performance can be made. The same criteria apply to the linkage timings – how long it takes to link to another process. Control and quality targets go across several processes – for example, both the incident and change management processes would need quality and control metrics. However, there will be some activities that do not have control and quality requirements. Remember that quality and performance are interlinked – changing one will affect the other.

A simple way to plan metrics is to create a process flow similar to Figure 2.20, entering the targets in the appropriate boxes.

■ **Identify and select tools** It is now necessary to go through our process and ask how the activities can be performed to meet the metrics specified in previous steps. Some of the tasks will only involve thinking, whereas others may involve quite sophisticated technology. The tools depend entirely upon the process that you have created. Wherever possible, a single solution for a process should be sought in order to reduce potential conflicts and costs. Work your way through the activities in sequence to identify technology requirements, and create a needs analysis from which you can select your technology solution. Remember to follow your organization's approved method for selecting and buying software. The final act in this step would be to purchase and implement the tools, following organizational rules and using change management.

- **Build and test the process** You are now ready to build your process by bringing together your documented process and the technology required to drive it. As this step will vary to such a degree from organization to organization it is impossible to provide any level of detail here, but remember to plan and test thoroughly.

- **Implement the process** Finally we are ready to implement the process. Again, this step will vary hugely, but it is essential to ensure that all staff who will be using the process are fully trained.

Building ITIL processes is a challenging task, but it can also be a very rewarding one. The detail of your processes will, to some degree, govern how long it will take to implement your ITIL Lite initiative. It pays to be frugal with documentation and remain focused on fitness for purpose. Don't forget to consult the relevant publications and, if there is a good process in there, use it – often there is software or hardware to support these processes, and it can be easier to change working practices than software.

Categorizing ITIL components

3

3 Categorizing ITIL components

ITIL is generally considered to consist of 26 processes and four functions. One of the major challenges facing an ITIL Lite implementation project is deciding which of these processes and functions to use, and which kind of project to build. Because there are so many processes and functions, it is possible for different organizations to build completely different systems, using different combinations of the ITIL components. Because ITIL is a framework (and not a methodology), different processes and functions can be selected to meet individual demands in this way.

When building your ITIL Lite project there are some obvious basic 'ingredients' but because there are so many components to choose from, the final project will be something quite individual – and even deciding on the basics can be tricky. The project will continue to develop beyond implementation and, as it matures, will change to meet demands.

Cooking with ITIL

Imagine that 10 first-class chefs were all given the same 30 ingredients from which to cook a main course of their choice. What would be the result? The answer is 10 excellent but very different meals. Unless the ingredients were extremely limited they would prepare a meal based on their skills, knowledge and taste. This is the dilemma facing everyone who starts implementing ITIL – which of the 30 ingredients do I use and which dish should I cook?

Cooking with ITIL v2 was much easier because we tended to use only ingredients from *Service Support* and *Service Delivery*. The fewer ingredients there are, the more likely it is that the chefs will cook the same meal. Certainly the decision will be easier and less skill and knowledge will be required. When choosing a new meal, most of us would consult a recipe, a book or the internet – maybe even a recipe created by one of our 10 first-class chefs. When implementing ITIL, we can learn from our top ITIL chefs through their books, web-support services, conferences, courses and complementary publications such as this one. We do not have a recipe book available for ITIL but with the help of this publication we can build our own recipe.

There are, of course, some basic ingredients that are used in most main course recipes – salt, pepper, herbs, butter, oil and flour etc. You are probably looking at the list and thinking that there are some basics we have missed. Not even the top chefs would agree on a set of basics without discussion and dispute. The same applies when selecting basic components. One of the ingredients for a main course could be the potato. Add to the potato some butter, a pinch of pepper, some chopped green onions and garlic, mash it all together and suddenly you have a different dish. Don't forget that, as the components mature, people will add their own flavourings to meet demand.

3.1 WHY DO ITIL COMPONENTS NEED TO BE CATEGORIZED?

With 30 processes and functions from which to choose, it's essential that criteria are established to reduce this list and help ensure that an ITIL Lite implementation project will provide excellent IT service management. It's easy to look at the processes and functions as one long list, without considering how they interface with each other, and why some are essential but need support from the others.

A game of ITIL

ITIL Lite is a bit like a game of football. Players on the field are taking part in the action, while the coaches are responsible for tactics, which influence the players. Depending upon the circumstances, the coaches may change tactics – but the players are responsible for actioning them. Arguably, the fans are also trying to influence the players' actions. But without resources such as the infrastructure (for example, the stadium) there would be no action to influence. Finally, the team requires underpinning, which would include financial support and investment. In essence, a good football team needs to operate on four levels – action, influencing, resourcing and underpinning (see Figure 3.1).

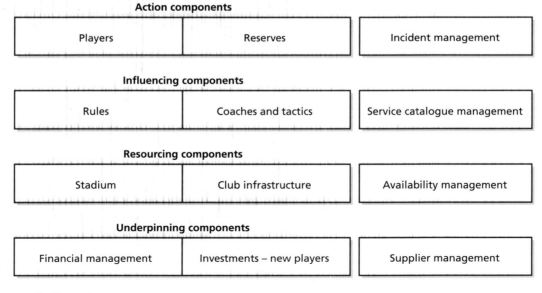

Figure 3.1 Football analogy

Incident management is our action example and service catalogue management our influencing one. Effectively, the incident process does not change but the actions of the staff designated to allocate priorities may be affected by service level agreements (SLAs). For example, priority allocation is based on an SLA so, every time a priority is allocated, an SLA will be behind the priority level allocated to the incident. In this manner, the football players are influenced by coaches and the tactics which they adopt.

Figure 3.1 shows that the stadium and club infrastructure provide the resourcing services to ensure that all is ready for the fans on match day. This involves making sure that it suits the needs of the team and is ready on time. Elsewhere, the club infrastructure ensures that all of the components required to manage a game are in place. The related component is availability management. The availability of services to an agreed level is a key role for ITSM. Resourcing provides the basis for the influencing factors – if the availability targets are altered, then the SLAs will need to be changed which will, in turn, influence the incident component (action).

The football team is underpinned by financial management and investment. The related ITIL component is supplier management, which underpins many IT activities. If the suppliers that underpin a contract are changed, the availability resource may have to be altered, which could mean that a new SLA needs to be created. This, in turn, may alter the actions for the incident management process.

It's important to categorize components to clarify how they fit together and provide an overall service to ITSM customers. We can, for example, survive

without service catalogues but still need incident management. Without SLAs, incident management may not be as effective but will still exist unless errors and questions from customers can be eliminated.

3.2 THE FOUR CATEGORIES

There are four different types of component – action, influencing, resourcing and underpinning:

- **Action components** These components require actions of an operational nature to be performed as part of their normal functionality. In addition they:
  - Are essential components because they cannot be removed – whether or not ITIL is followed, incidents, problems and changes will still occur
  - Include operational activities – for example, utilizing a workaround to resolve an incident, or providing a command to start a service
  - Are performed on a regular, scheduled basis
  - Can cause problems (e.g. system outages) if they are not performed correctly.

  Action components are at the front end of IT. They are dynamic and have an instant impact. They can be, and often are, automated – for example, automatically starting and closing a service at set dates and times.
- **Influencing components** These modify and influence the way that action components perform their actions. They are important because they:
  - Provide the terms and conditions for the action category
  - Provide the parameters for the action category, e.g. SLAs

- Work with the business community to ensure that IT requirements are being met
- Maintain the IT infrastructure and configuration of the infrastructure
- Monitor and measure service commitments.
■ **Resourcing components** These ensure that the other components have the resources to meet their service commitments. Resourcing components could also be described as being responsible for the IT environment because they must ensure that:
  - There are sufficient resources to support IT services
  - There will be sufficient resources to support new, and the growth of current, IT services
  - Service availability is measured and provided
  - The transition of services is managed and performed.

■ **Underpinning components** These provide the underpinning facilities required by all components. Some of these components, such as financial management, may also serve other areas of IT. The underpinning components work across all services and systems to provide:
  - Sufficient financial resources and service
  - Forward and strategy planning
  - Management of suppliers, outsourcers and contracts
  - Management of the complete service portfolio, which underpins all IT services.

The four categories are simple to understand and provide perspective when building an ITIL Lite implementation project. They allow us to select the most appropriate components and help us understand how those components should interface with each other.

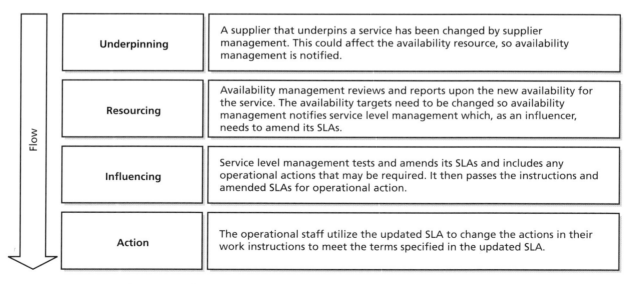

Figure 3.2 Four categories example

Some of the components can fit into more than one category – for example, capacity management can be a planning function (resourcing) or an operational function (action) by entering commands to increase capacity. If this is the case, then you must decide which category features most prominently in the components.

As an example, Figure 3.2 demonstrates how the categories link together when a new supplier (e.g. a software vendor or an outsourcer) is contracted to provide services to IT. It shows how the different categories interrelate to each other to provide an end-to-end service (in this case the adoption of a new supplier).

3.2.1 Components for the action category

Selecting some of the action components is simple because they are unequivocal, whereas others depend very much upon local interpretation. Ten of the 30 ITIL processes and functions are action components, all of which come from the *ITIL Service Operation* and *ITIL Service Transition* publications – unsurprising given that the very titles of these publications suggest that they contain action components. The 10 components (as shown in Figure 3.3) are as follows:

- **Service desk** Service desks can perform many actions in a day – from managing complex technical incidents to handling more mundane tasks (such as password resets). Either way, most of these incidents will require some actions to be performed. According to *ITIL Service Operation* the primary objective of the service desk is to 'provide a single point of contact between the services being provided and the users'. The service desk follows incident management and request fulfilment to 'restore the normal-state service operation to the users as quickly as possible' which could involve 'fixing a technical fault … fulfilling a service request or answering a query – anything that is needed to allow the users to return to working satisfactorily'. You may, of course, have a help desk that primarily takes and escalates calls and this escalation will be part of the overall action to get the service working.
  Verdict: an action component

- **Incident management** In most organizations incident management is performed by the service desk, which almost makes it an action component by default. ITIL states that incident management has 'the ability to detect and resolve incidents' (*ITIL Service Operation*). To achieve this it must be able to perform actions or work with those who will provide actions.

Service desk	Event management	Request fulfilment	Service asset and configuration management
Incident management	Change management	IT operations management (control and facilities)	
Problem management	Release and deployment management	Access management	

Figure 3.3 Action category components

Every IT organization is performing incident management – whether as a formal process or a series of ad hoc events.

Verdict: an action component

■ **Problem management** This is more contentious because it can be a function that identifies, reports and monitors the progress of removing problems but does not take any direct action. As such, it could belong to the influencing category because it will influence how the service and incident management function. However, in many cases, problem management enlists other groups to enter the correct data to remove faults and, if it is the job of problem management to oversee and check these changes, then it is an operational unit.

Verdict: an action component but could be an influencing component

■ **Event management** Event management is defined in *ITIL Service Operation* as 'the process that monitors all events that occur through the IT infrastructure to allow for normal operation and also to detect and escalate exceptional conditions'. 'Escalate' is, in itself, an action which, if not performed correctly, could result in an unscheduled outage. *ITIL Service Operation* goes on to state that the ability 'to detect events, make sense of them and determine the appropriate control action is coordinated by the event management process'. Depending upon the circumstances, event management may well take the appropriate action. The same arguments pertaining to problem management exist here – event management could be an administrative task and, as such, an influencing component.

Verdict: an action component but could be an influencing component

■ **Change management** At first, change management could be considered an influencing component because it does not carry out many, if any, of the actions required to perform changes. However, this is misleading because the people who are performing the changes are temporary employees of change management when they are performing the change actions. It is change management, and not those making the changes, who are responsible for failed changes. It is the role of change management to approve and check all the actions performed during a change. They are supervisors of the change. In addition, many change requests will come from the influencing category. You may decide that change fits into the influencing category, but remember one of its main roles is action control.

Verdict: an action component but could be an influencing component

■ **Release and deployment management** This is a clear action component. According to *ITIL Service Transition,* the purpose of release and deployment management is 'to plan, schedule and control the build, test and deployment of releases, and to deliver new functionality required by the business while protecting the integrity of existing services'. In this case, the word 'deployment' means that a series of actions needs to be performed.

Verdict: an action component

■ **Request fulfilment** The main role of request fulfilment is to manage and handle service requests (such as a request to change a password). It is designed to reduce the congestion of incident and change management. Service requests occur frequently and are low risk, which is why they are not in the change management process. The activities in the request fulfilment process differ dramatically from one organization to the next, as can be seen by the roles of help desks and service desks in request fulfilment: e.g. request fulfilment can range from just being an administration post to taking direct actions to fulfil the requests within request fulfilment. Therefore, request fulfilment could be an action component or an influencing component, depending upon its local responsibilities. It is rare, however, to find a request fulfilment function that does not take some level of operational action, e.g. to change a password on request.

Verdict: an action component but, in rare circumstances, could be an influencing component

■ **IT operations management (controls and facilities)** This is the stage of the lifecycle where plans are implemented. The key point is that the plan was not created here. This is a strong action component, especially when considering some of the actions undertaken by operations management: console management, job scheduling, backup, restore, print and output management.

Verdict: an action component

■ **Access management** This is another tricky component to assess. *ITIL Service Operation* states that 'access management is a process that is executed by all technical and application management functions and is not usually a separate function. However, there is likely to be a single control point of coordination, usually in IT operations management or on the service desk.' You could discuss this component all day and still not agree where it fits. The key phrase here is 'control point' – which would require actions to maintain safe access control. The answer lies in how access management is applied if it updates

access data – if it blocks a user, it's definitely an action component. However, if it's evaluating access risks, then it's an influencing component.

Verdict: an action component but could be an influencing component

■ **Service asset and configuration management** According to *ITIL Service Transition* one of the main objectives of service asset and configuration management is to 'identify, control, record, report, audit and verify services and other configuration items (CIs), including versions, baselines, constituent components, their attributes and relationships'. How can you perform these tasks without performing some actions?

Verdict: an action component

The litmus test for a component in the action category is what would happen if that component was not performed, or not performed correctly. If the answer is that there would be failures, delays, outages, lost business time, missed availability etc. then it should reside in the action category. All of the components discussed in this section certainly meet those criteria.

3.2.2 Components for the influencing category

Like the action components, the influencing components do not come from all five ITIL 2011 editions; three of them come from *ITIL Service Transition* and two each from *ITIL Service Design* and *ITIL Continual Service Improvement*.

Identifying the influencing components is fairly straightforward because of their relationship to many of the action components. In addition, they often play the role of a go-between, linking the resourcing components to the action components.

Service level management	Service catalogue management	The seven-step improvement process
Service validation and testing	Change evaluation	Knowledge management

Figure 3.4 Influencing category components

The six components (as shown in Figure 3.4) are as follows:

■ **Service level management** The overall goal of service level management is to ensure that an agreed level of service is being provided for all current and future IT services, but it does not perform the actions to meet these goals. One of the objectives of service level management, as outlined in *ITIL Service Design*, is to 'define, document, agree, monitor, measure, report and review the level of IT services provided'. If this criterion is not being met then service level management will probably notify IT operations management who, in turn, may have to change its actions accordingly. You could merge service level management and IT operations management and create a new function. If you do, then you will need to decide whether this component is to be an action or an influencing component. If it remains as one component, then it is an influencing component.
Verdict: an influencing component

■ **Service validation and testing** Confusingly, service validation and testing will include some operational and action activities, but these will be performed in the background and should not affect the daily services provided to the customers. Service validation and testing is about quality assurance, 'establishing that the service design and release will deliver a new or changed service or service offering that is fit for purpose

and fit for use' (*ITIL Service Transition*). The key term here is 'fit for purpose', because this is where the new services are created and tested.
Verdict: an influencing component

■ **Service catalogue management** This is one of the more obvious influencing components because the service catalogue contains many of the criteria that govern how the action processes are performed. *ITIL Service Design* recommends that 'a service portfolio containing a service catalogue is produced and maintained to provide a central, accurate set of information on all services and to develop a service-focused culture'. Service catalogues are the influencers because the action processes are expected to deliver the conditions described in the SLAs. In short, it is the prime influencer for the action processes.
Verdict: an influencing component

■ **Change evaluation** As its name suggests, evaluation is about making sure the performance of a new or changed service is acceptable and achievable. This process is key to the success of change management. During change evaluation, the 'actual performance of a change is assessed against its predicted performance' (*ITIL Service Transition*). The current performance will be supplied by the action components and the changed performance will be supported by the action processes. The results of evaluation can have a tremendous influence on the action processes, especially when new services are being evaluated.

Verdict: an influencing component

■ **Knowledge management** This can be a vast subject but it has a clear purpose which, according to *ITIL Service Transition*, is to 'share perspectives, ideas, experience and information; to ensure that these are available in the right place at the right time to enable informed decisions; and to improve efficiency by reducing the need to rediscover knowledge'. This would suggest that it is an influencing component, because the only actions taken are to update the knowledge, which is not directly affecting the daily service delivery. The information management by knowledge management will clearly influence the actions taken by the action components.

Verdict: an influencing component

■ **The seven-step improvement process** This is a rather nebulous component because, until you know what needs improving, it is difficult to embark on a service improvement plan (SIP) unless you undertake proactive monitoring and analysis. Typically, SIPs and continual service improvement concentrate on putting into place corrective measures and service innovations, rather than performing operational actions. However, it is easy to imagine how the implementation of a SIP could affect operational actions.

Verdict: an influencing component

The influencing components are vital to the current and ongoing success, or failure, of IT service management because operational actions can only be successful if the targets, objectives, deliverables and customer requirements are known and met. A note of caution: the influencers should always be aware of the capabilities of the technology and services available to the operational teams.

3.2.3 Components for the resourcing category

The resourcing category is unique among the four categories because it is the only one to span all five ITIL publications.

Demand management comes from *ITIL Service Strategy*, availability and capacity management from *ITIL Service Design*, transition planning and support from *ITIL Service Transition*, and application and technical management from *ITIL Service Operation*. This is because resourcing is crucial in providing the standards of service required to meet agreed service levels. No matter how smart you are you cannot deliver services without the resources. The six components (as shown in Figure 3.5) are as follows:

■ **Capacity management** ITSM and managing the capacity required to support ITSM services is like being on a constant diet trying to balance your calories, exercise, water intake and your wardrobe! Similarly, capacity management

Capacity management	Transition planning and support	Application management
Availability management	Demand management	Technical management

Figure 3.5 Resourcing category components

must juggle disk capacity, memory capacity, server capacity, telecommunications capacity and workstation capacity etc. According to *ITIL Service Design*, the purpose of capacity management is 'to ensure that the capacity of IT services and the IT infrastructure meets the agreed capacity- and performance-related requirements in a cost-effective and timely manner'. The primary objective is to make sure that capacity is fit for purpose now, and in the foreseeable future. Having the right amount of capacity resource available requires analysis and planning as an ongoing activity. Although without capacity management there would soon be customer service problems, most of the updates identified by capacity management are subjected to change management, where the operational actions will take place. It is possible that staff performing capacity management could take some actions – for example, if they see a threshold being threatened they may release some resources from elsewhere. In fact, some of these actions can be automated. These are valid actions but usually workarounds and not regular operational actions.

Verdict: a resourcing component

■ **Availability management** This is very similar in nature to capacity management. Availability management, according to *ITIL Service Design*, 'provides a point of focus and management for all availability-related issues, relating to both services and resources, ensuring that availability targets in all areas are measured and achieved'. As with capacity management, it may be necessary, at times, to take instant action to remedy an availability issue. But, just like capacity management, these are workarounds rather than regular operational actions.

Verdict: a resourcing component

■ **Transition planning and support** Transition planning and support is a key component that is often forgotten or overlooked. It is the lynchpin between four of the ITIL publications – *ITIL Service Strategy*, *ITIL Service Design*, *ITIL Service Operation* and *ITIL Service Transition*. This last publication outlines the objectives of transition planning and support, one of which is to 'plan and coordinate the resources to ensure that the requirements of service strategy encoded in service design are effectively realized in service operation'. In addition, the process should 'identify, manage and control risks, to minimize the chance of failure and disruption across transition activities'. As this implies, the role of transition planning and support is to control the risks of failure and disruption. To do this, it has to make sure that all of the resources are in place. Capacity management is concerned with capacity, availability management with availability, but it is transition planning and support that ensures that these, and other components, are all ready on time when transitioning a new service. In short, transition planning and support is a resourcing component because it is the control point for the other resourcing components.

Verdict: a resourcing component

■ **Application management** Application management is responsible for managing applications throughout their lifecycle and will, therefore, touch on all four categories at some point. *ITIL Service Operation* indicates that application management belongs to the resourcing category: 'it provides the actual resources to support the service lifecycle. In this role, application management ensures that resources are effectively trained and deployed to design, build, transition, operate, and improve the technology required to deliver and support IT services.' Hidden in the middle of this quote is the word 'operate', which indicates that application management could also be an action component. So does it belong to the action or resource category? The answer lies in how application management is approached. Typically, most of the operational activities for an application will be performed by IT operations management, which is an action component. If this is the case, then application management is clearly a resourcing component.

Verdict: a resourcing component

- **Demand management** In ITIL v2, demand management was part of capacity management because it is 'responsible for understanding, anticipating and influencing customer demand for services' (ITIL Glossary). So demand identifies the requirements for a service, while capacity management provides the resources and performance to meet those demands. Capacity and demand are so closely linked that it is difficult to separate them. So, wherever you place capacity, you should also place demand.

Verdict: a resourcing component

- **Technical management** 'It provides the actual resources to support the service lifecycle. In this role technical management ensures that resources are effectively trained and deployed to design, build, transition, operate and improve the technology required to deliver and support IT services.' This quote should look familiar – it is the same one from *ITIL Service Operation* used in the explanation of application management, with just the word 'application' transposed for 'technical'. This is because they work so closely together, with technical management providing the technology to support the applications. As in application management, most of the operational activities identified by technical

management are typically performed by IT operations management, which is an action component. Given this, technical management is clearly a resourcing component.

Verdict: a resourcing component

3.2.4 Components for the underpinning category

Components in the underpinning category provide services across a wide range of the other categories and, as such, underpin their activities. In fact, some of these are so important that they may be managed outside ITSM because they also underpin the rest of IT, and even some business activities – such as financial management.

The components in the underpinning category are from the *ITIL Service Strategy* and *ITIL Service Design* publications. Underpinning cannot be performed at the end of a lifecycle – it needs to be at the front end, where it can provide some of the foundations for the other components. The eight components (as shown in Figure 3.6) are as follows:

- **Financial management for IT services** Financial management is essential. Without it, no projects could be implemented. The ITIL glossary (**www. best-management-practice.com/Glossaries- and-Acronyms**) defines financial management as the 'function and processes responsible for managing an IT service provider's budgeting, accounting and charging requirements'. Financial management underpins every other ITIL process and function. Sometimes the control of financial management for ITSM may reside in another department, e.g. a central IT FM unit, or the corporate FM department – either way it is a vital underpinning function.

Verdict: an underpinning component

Financial management for IT services	Strategy management for IT services	Information security management	Business relationship management
IT service continuity management	Service portfolio management	Supplier management	Design coordination

Figure 3.6 Underpinning category components

■ **IT service continuity management** It is the value to the business that makes IT service continuity management so important as an underpinning component. It is like an IT insurance policy – we need to invest in IT service continuity management, but hope that we don't get value for money from the investment. Just like health insurance, we might spend the money but hope that we don't have to use it. The purpose of IT service continuity management is 'to support the overall business continuity management (BCM) process by ensuring that, by managing the risks that could seriously affect IT services, the IT service provider can always provide minimum agreed business continuity-related service levels' (*ITIL Service Design*). The key thing to remember is that this does not only apply to the services and applications available to the business community, but also to IT services and applications – for example, IT service continuity management should make sure that contingency plans are in place for the service desk in case a fire eliminates the service desk environment. Just like financial management, sometimes the control of IT service continuity management resides in another department (e.g. a central IT department unit or a corporate IT service continuity management department); either way it is a vital underpinning function.
Verdict: an underpinning component

■ **Strategy management for IT services** Rather than launch into a description of strategy management for IT services, it is easier to quote from *ITIL Service Strategy*: 'Strategy management for IT services is the process responsible for defining and maintaining an organization's perspective, position, plans and patterns with regard to its services and the management of those services. The purpose of a service strategy is to articulate how a service provider will enable an organization to achieve its business outcomes.' Strategy management for IT services is the key to success for many organizations. The better the strategy and the more clearly defined it is, the more the other ITSM processes can deliver their services in a manner that is fit for purpose. For this reason strategy management for IT services is clearly an underpinning component.
Verdict: an underpinning component

■ **Service portfolio management** Service portfolio management is an important component because it defines and describes all of the services provided by IT. It 'considers services in terms of the business value that they provide' (ITIL Glossary). A service portfolio is 'the complete set of services that is managed by a service provider. The service portfolio is used to manage the entire lifecycle of all services. It includes three categories of service: service pipeline (proposed or in development), service catalogue (live or available for deployment) and retired services' (*ITIL Service Strategy*). Service portfolio management could be described as omnipresent as far as ITSM is concerned and, as such, is an underpinning component.

Verdict: an underpinning component

■ **Information security management** Security management is essential to any organization, but here it applies specifically to service management information. The purpose of the information security management (ISM) process, as described in *ITIL Service Design*, is to 'align IT security with business security and ensure that the confidentiality, integrity and availability of the organization's assets, information, data and IT services always matches the agreed needs of the business'. The level of security obviously depends upon the services being provided to the business, but each of the ITIL components is subjected to ISM and, for this reason, it is an underpinning component. Just like financial management and IT service continuity management, control of ISM may sometimes reside in another department (e.g. a central IT department unit or a corporate ISM department) but either way it is a vital underpinning component.

Verdict: an underpinning component

■ **Supplier management** Supplier management is concerned with the ongoing relationship with a supplier and the management of the quality of services that they provide. The negotiating and financial components could also be handled here, or you may have a specialized contract management facility or department. Either way, to be successful, supplier management must deliver its goal, as set out in *ITIL Service Design*: 'to obtain value for money from suppliers and to provide seamless quality of IT service to the business by ensuring that all contracts and agreements with suppliers support the needs of the business and that all suppliers meet their contractual commitments'. Some of the suppliers will underpin numerous services, while others may only underpin one service. In some cases, they may underpin a whole component or two – for example, you may outsource your service desk along with incident management, in which case you still have these action components in place but they are underpinned by suppliers.

Verdict: an underpinning component

■ **Business relationship management** Business relationship management works to establish and maintain a business relationship at two levels – between the business and the IT service providers – so that services are fit for purpose. To this end business relationship management is constantly in touch with both the business and ITSM, but on a planning level rather than a practical operational level. It therefore provides a vital strategic service to IT and, in particular, ITSM. Categorizing business relationship management can be quite difficult because, more than any other process or function, it will visit all four categories at some time. However, most business relationship management time will be spent working with the business and translating its needs into ITSM.

Verdict: an underpinning component

■ **Design coordination** This is a crucial component because the wrong design can be both very expensive and result in an inferior service being supplied by ITSM. Taking a complex and diverse set of conditions and people and turning this into a pure-gold service is almost like alchemy. The processes of application management and technical management depend heavily upon design coordination to provide the necessary guidance and information from which they can construct services and applications.

Verdict: an underpinning component

Some components can be particularly problematic, and there is no predefined way in which to approach them – this is why different people may categorize them in different ways. It is highly likely that when building your ITIL Lite project, you will place some of these components in different categories. That doesn't matter. What does matter is that you put time and effort into categorizing your components. A quick glance at the component category chart (Figure 3.7) shows how the components take on a different perspective once they are compared on the chart. Notice that the components are fairly evenly distributed between the categories. This is a good sign, showing that the components make a well-balanced structure. This is why ITIL has been so successful.

Figure 3.8 shows how the categories are distributed across the ITIL publications but, more importantly, also illustrates why you cannot implement

Action components			
Service desk	Event management	Request fulfilment	Service asset and configuration management
Incident management	Change management	IT operations management (control and facilities)	
Problem management	Release and deployment management	Access management	

Influencing components		
Service level management	Service catalogue management	The seven-step improvement process
Service validation and testing	Change evaluation	Knowledge management

Resourcing components		
Capacity management	Transition planning and support	Application management
Availability management	Demand management	Technical management

Underpinning components			
Financial management for IT services	Strategy management for IT services	Information security management	Business relationship management
IT service continuity management	Service portfolio management	Supplier management	Design coordination

Figure 3.7 Typical component categories

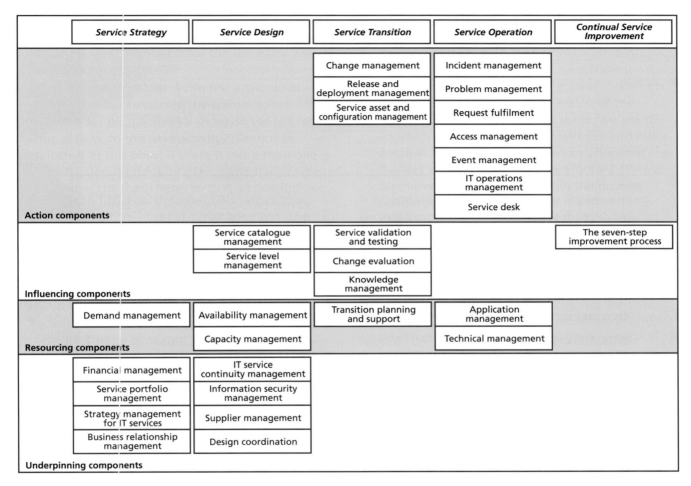

	Service Strategy	Service Design	Service Transition	Service Operation	Continual Service Improvement
Action components			Change management	Incident management	
			Release and deployment management	Problem management	
			Service asset and configuration management	Request fulfilment	
				Access management	
				Event management	
				IT operations management	
				Service desk	
Influencing components		Service catalogue management	Service validation and testing		The seven-step improvement process
		Service level management	Change evaluation		
			Knowledge management		
Resourcing components	Demand management	Availability management	Transition planning and support	Application management	
		Capacity management		Technical management	
Underpinning components	Financial management	IT service continuity management			
	Service portfolio management	Information security management			
	Strategy management for IT services	Supplier management			
	Business relationship management	Design coordination			

Figure 3.8 Category to publication template

the processes in a linear fashion, starting with *ITIL Service Strategy* and moving through the publications – unless you want to leave your action components until last.

3.3   THE ART OF CATEGORIZATION

Categorization identifies and agrees the prime category for each ITIL component. This is essential if we are to build an ITIL Lite project that is balanced and relevant.

3.3.1 Reasons for categorization

Categorization is important for many reasons, including:

- **To fully understand the role of each component** Do not reject any of the components at this stage. In order to fully understand their scope, role and the part that they could play in a customized ITIL facility you should review, discuss and categorize every component.

- **To agree perception** Another reason not to reject any components at this stage is to ensure that perception reflects reality. In other words, a component may be perceived as an action component by one faction of IT, but an influencing component by another. This is a discrepancy that must be resolved. It is possible that both perceptions have some validity, but the primary category needs to be established.

- **To ensure that you understand the role of each ITIL component** To categorize a component you will have to review and understand its role before you can decide its prime category. This can be a quick and interesting way of learning more about ITIL.

- **To ensure a well-balanced result** Balancing is important because if you have too much emphasis on one category you will not provide a good service. This will become very important later on, when deciding which components to keep and which to eliminate.

- **To gain a more logical view of ITIL** ITIL is constructed using a lifecycle approach, which is very effective and relates to how we should support our customers. The process of categorization will help to emphasize the lifecycle philosophy.

The intention, at this stage, is not to eliminate components. However, there may be some that you eliminate at this stage because they are either not within the scope of ITSM, or they are owned elsewhere – for example, financial management. However, before rejecting a component, it's still important to review its scope and role, and to discuss it with the current owners.

3.3.2 Guidance for categorization

Categorization is unique to each organization and will be carried out according to the organization's needs. This is because ITIL is intended to be used as a framework, and no two organizations are the same. Flexibility is encouraged but there are some basic rules that should aid successful categorization:

- **Keep an open mind** It is inevitable that there will be some debate when deciding which category applies to a component, so it is important to always keep an open mind.

- **Focus on the prime category** Although you will need to discuss all of the potential categories for a component, remember that it is the prime category that matters.

- **Ensure component comprehension** It is important that any participants involved in the categorization understand the ITIL scope, and the role of these components. This may require background reading and, in some cases, further education on ITIL.

- **Focus on ITIL** Although you will need to keep in mind your current status, remember that it is the ITIL components that we are categorizing and not your current functions. Try to remain focused on the future, and not on the present.

The sweet smell of ITIL

What else has thousands of potential ingredients that can be selected and integrated to produce a unique result? Just think of all the potential natural smells that are blended to make a perfume. Don't think that you can just keep mixing smells until you've found a nice one – it's a lot more scientific than that. In fact, just like ITIL, there are four categories:

■ **Primary scents** These consist of one or a few main ingredients for a certain concept, such as 'rose'. It is also possible to create an abstract primary scent that does not bear a resemblance to a natural ingredient – such as cola. Often the choice of a primary scent is influenced by the target recipient. These become the essential elements around which the perfume will be based, and they are key to its success. From this basic data, the process of perfume creation can begin. Just like ITIL action components, the primary scents provide the foundation for success.

■ **Modifiers** Modifiers are ingredients that alter the primary scent to give the perfume a certain desired character – for instance, fruit scents may be included in a floral primary to create a fruity floral aroma. Also, the abstract cola flavour could have a cherry scent added to create a cherry cola smell. If only primary scents were used, then there would be much less choice. The skill of the perfume master is in the subtle addition that creates a new and exciting combination. The ITIL influencing components are similar to the perfume modifiers. For example, service level management and its SLAs 'modify' incident management actions.

■ **Blenders** This is a large group of ingredients that smooth out the transitions of a perfume between different 'layers' or bases. Their main role is to round out, smooth or harmonize the primary and modifying fragrances. Like the perfume blenders, capacity and availability blend the service into a cohesive and efficient facility.

■ **Resource** This is used to support the primary scent by bolstering and fixing it. Resins, wood scents and amber bases are among the scents typically used for fixative purposes. Without these components, smells can break apart and not work, like immiscible liquids. The perfume resource is just like the underpinning components.

3.3.3 Performing categorization

A key objective of categorization is to produce a categorization chart and document the main reasons for the categories allocated to the ITIL components. To perform categorization and produce a map, the steps outlined in Figure 3.9 need to be carried out as an action plan.

Most of the steps shown in Figure 3.9 are logical, but still need to be performed. It may be tempting to cut corners, but this must be avoided.

■ **Step 1 – create a team** This can be a small team with good connections. Because, in a later step, the component categorizations will be distributed it is not necessary to have a large group with representatives from all quarters of IT. Instead, the team should consist of representatives from your key ITSM facilities. An ideal number of team members would be four – enough to get different viewpoints but not too many to delay or complicate the action plan.

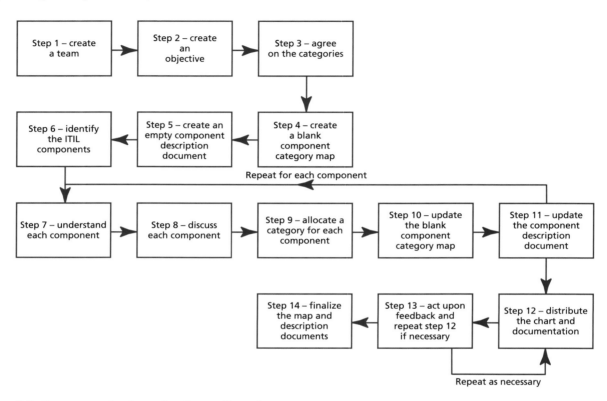

Figure 3.9 Component categorization action plan

■ **Step 2 – create an objective** It is important to quantify the reasons that will drive your ITIL Lite component categorization. The first task for the categorization team is to agree and document the objectives for categorization. The objective could be as simple as 'to review each of the ITIL components, decide which will be the prime category for each component and document the reasons'.

■ **Step 3 – agree on the categories** In this publication we have suggested four categories – action, influencing, resourcing and underpinning – but these are flexible. You may decide to adopt all of these as they are described here,

or you may want to remove a category or two, or change the objectives of a category etc. The deliverable from this step should be a list of the categories that you intend to use and the objectives for each of those categories.

■ **Step 4 – create a blank component category map** This a slight misnomer because this step really involves selecting the tool. The map is quite simple and can be created using Microsoft Word or PowerPoint. You can also decide upon the style and layout at this stage. You can use Figure 3.7 as a guide.

■ **Step 5 – create an empty component description document** The component description document is very easy to create (electronically, in a spreadsheet) but it's important to carefully consider the contents. We suggest at least four columns (see Figure 3.10). The 'component' column contains the component name, the 'ITIL publication' column contains the ITIL 2011 edition reference point for readers of the document, the 'category' column contains the selected prime category and, finally, the 'reason' column contains the reason for selecting the prime category. For illustration purposes, we have included in Figure 3.10 a quote from *ITIL Service Operation* but there is no reason why you cannot use your own quotes if you wish.

■ **Step 6 – identify the ITIL components** This is an important step, and it's essential that no components are omitted at this stage. It is generally recognized that ITIL is made up of four functions and 26 processes and these 30 components, at least, should be included at this stage.

There are other components which fall outside this list but are included in the publications:

● Requirements engineering (*ITIL Service Design*)
● Data and information management (*ITIL Service Design*)
● Operational activities in other lifecycle phases (*ITIL Service Operation*)
● Return on investment for CSI (*ITIL Continual Service Improvement*)
● Business questions for CSI (*ITIL Continual Service Improvement*).

It is also worth considering these additional components at this stage. Use the contents tables in the publications to highlight any possible additions to your list of components.

Component	ITIL publication	Category	Reason
Service desk	*ITIL Service Operation*	Action	'The primary aim of the service desk is to provide a single point of contact between the services being provided and the users ... Service desk staff execute the incident management and request fulfilment processes to restore the normal-state service operation to the users as quickly as possible. In this context 'restoration of service' is meant in the widest possible sense. While this could involve fixing a technical fault, it could equally involve fulfilling a service request or answering a query – anything that is needed to allow the users to return to working satisfactorily.' (*ITIL Service Operation*)

Figure 3.10 Component description document

■ **Step 7 – understand each component** As Figure 3.9 shows, steps 7 to 11 are repeated for each component. Before a decision can be made concerning the category of a component, the team members must first understand that component by reading the appropriate section in the ITIL publication. This is necessary even if you have attended an ITIL Foundation course.

■ **Step 8 – discuss each component** Once the category is understood, the next step is for the team to discuss the component, focusing on which category it should fall under. Try to steer away from discussing whether it will be included in your ITIL Lite structure – this can be debated later.

■ **Step 9 – allocate a category for each component** After discussion, the team must allocate a category for each component.

■ **Step 10 – update the blank component category map** Enter the appropriate data into your component category map.

■ **Step 11 – update the component description document** Enter the appropriate data into your component description document.

■ **Step 12 – distribute your chart and documentation** Once you have worked through all the components, distribute the results to key ITSM staff for their comments.

■ **Step 13 – act upon feedback and repeat step 12 if necessary** Any feedback should be reviewed and, if required, you may need to backtrack the action plan to change a category or a description of a category. If you do make a change as a result of feedback you must repeat step 12.

■ **Step 14 – finalize the map and description documents** Lastly, you should issue a final copy of the documentation, ensuring that all parties understand the category allocations and the logic behind those allocations.

This is a simple set of action points, but it is an interesting exercise from which all team members should emerge with a greater knowledge of ITIL and its components. Learning by involvement is one of the quickest ways to understand a subject.

3.4 SUMMARY

ITIL has been designed to provide a balance between all of its components, so it's important to ensure that, if you eliminate any of those components, the status quo of ITIL is maintained. If not, a situation may develop where there is, for example, too much action and not enough influence.

The filtering process

4

4 The filtering process

Once we have categorized our ITIL processes and functions the next step is filtering. Selecting ITIL Lite components requires several levels of filtration. It is, of course, very subjective and needs care and attention.

4.1 FILTERING THE ITIL COMPONENTS

The first stage of filtering is to grade the components. Three levels of filtering are recommended – essential, rejected and potential:

- **Essential grade** These are the basic ITIL components that must be included in your Lite version of ITIL. If you have identified your reasons and approaches for not adopting full ITIL implementation, the essential grade processes should be easily isolated. Having identified all of the ITIL processes and functions, simply ask whether each component should be included in your version of ITIL Lite. Only include those that have an unequivocal 'yes' vote – the potentials and maybes will be addressed at another level of filtering. There are some triggers that can help you identify the essential grade components:
  - **The key service management trinity** Incident, problem and change are standard vital components and should be included in every service management offering.
  - **Existing components** If you already have a component, or components, in place before embarking on the ITIL Lite project, then they should automatically be included. It may be

that existing components do not reach the requirements specified by ITIL, but this is a concern for implementation, not selection.
  - **Tool capabilities** This may not seem a truly professional approach but it may be that you already have a tool that includes a number of ITIL components, not all of which are being utilized. For example, you may have a tool that you used for incident and change management that also has the capability to provide support for event management. In this case, you may consider event management an essential component. Be careful here that you do not allow available tools and technologies to dominate your ITIL Lite approach, though. The components supported by these tools are good candidates, but they must also meet the other criteria.
  - **Dependencies** Many of the components are interdependent and, for this reason, so are many of the processes. For example, service asset and configuration management prefers that change management is in place as a policing agent. In other words, you could have change management without service asset and configuration management, but not the other way around. When you have made your choice of components double-check that all of the dependent components have been included as essential components.
  - **Reasons for not implementing ITIL** Reject any components that do not gel with your reasons (see section 1.1).

- **Integration function** This is very similar to 'dependencies', above, except that these components link together two, or more, of the essential components that have been selected. Once the components have been selected, ensure that all of the integrator components have been included as 'essential'.

■ **Rejected grade** Rather than looking for an unequivocal 'yes', this grade of filtering is looking for a 'no'. Any potentials or maybes are left to be considered at a later stage, but anything that is definitely a 'no' is resigned to the rejected grade. At the end of this stage, there should be a list of essential components, rejected components and potential components.

■ **Potential grade** This is the most difficult level of filtering. In order to decide what components should or should not be included, it is wise to begin by assessing the validity of the negative comments before applying benefits criteria. If you still cannot make a decision you should:

- Ask all of those involved in this level of grading to make a list of the positive and negative points for each of the disputed components
- Collate all of these points and distribute them to all interested parties (i.e. all those that would be affected by these components if they were/were not to be included in ITIL Lite)
- Obtain feedback from the interested parties and distribute that feedback
- Arrange a meeting to decide which of the potential components will be implemented
- If in real doubt, you could suspend the doubtful component, or components, until the essential grade components have been implemented.

Remember that the potential grades can easily be omitted at a later stage, because they are not essential in creating your ITIL Lite template.

Figure 4.1 is a simple step-by-step procedure for carrying out the filtering process:

■ **Step 1 – decide grading levels** We have given the example of essential, potential and rejected grading levels. However, you may decide that more (or indeed fewer) grades are required.

■ **Step 2 – ensure that all relevant components are included** We have already discussed the fact that there could be some extra components that you would like to consider (see section 3.3.3, step 6). At this stage, investigate whether any additional relevant components are required, and update your component list as necessary.

■ **Step 3 – review your reasons** You are not expected to change your reasons here but you may want to add other reasons, ones which may have emerged as you've progressed through the previous planning stages. The reasons are the criteria around which you base the filters for your grading, so you should review them here and ensure that they are applied to all of the components.

■ **Step 4 – filter for the essential components** The objective of this step is obvious but may require some discussion and diplomacy before a list of essential components is finalized.

■ **Step 5 – filter for subsequent levels** If you didn't add any extra grading levels in step 1 then at the end of this step your filtering process will be complete. Because you have filtered out any rejected grades, the remaining components will be the potential grade components.

■ **Step 6 – document and distribute** The results of filtering are now distributed to a wider audience. There are numerous ways to distribute your

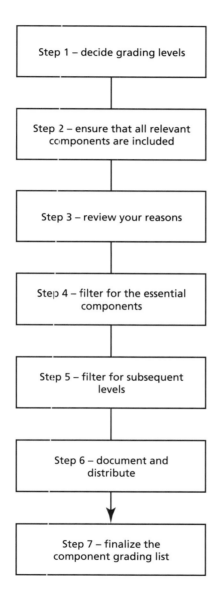

Figure 4.1 *Component grading plan*

filtered components, but a face-to-face approach works best – this way you know that others fully understand how the components have been filtered and it also allows feedback to be collated immediately.

■ **Step 7 – finalize the component grading list**
Collate and analyse the feedback. Depending upon the comments, you may decide to make some changes to your graded components list, in which case the list may need to be redistributed. Either way, a final version of the graded components list should now be produced.

ITIL Lite templates

5

5 ITIL Lite templates

Once you have filtered your components you are ready to take those components and use them to build an ITIL Lite template. This requires an approach (see Figure 5.1).

Example A in Figure 5.1 shows that the reason for implementing ITIL Lite is cost. This has been matched against service support as the approach. This example is not unusual. After all, most organizations that implemented ITIL v2 only implemented *Service Support* and a limited amount from *Service Delivery* because of financial restrictions. Example B shows an organization that has already implemented v2 and wants to manage their costs. They are therefore looking to upgrade their current v2 status and have chosen the v2 approach. There can be more than one reason for choosing a Lite approach, but only one template.

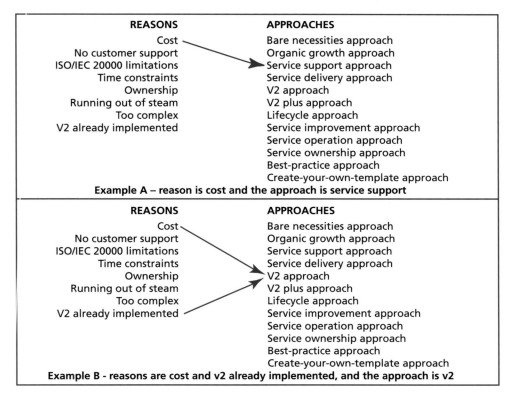

Figure 5.1 Reason and approach matching

Figure 5.1 summarizes the reasons and approaches but, of course, you may have different reasons which, in turn, require different approaches. Either way, it is recommended that you identify your reasons first and then identify the best approach, because this will influence what processes will be included in your ITIL Lite project.

To successfully build your version of ITIL Lite you will need to create a template which illustrates the components that you intend to include and their relationship to each other.

Figure 5.2 is a simple template, which allows the balance of an approach to be established. Reading from left to right, you can see how each ITIL 2011

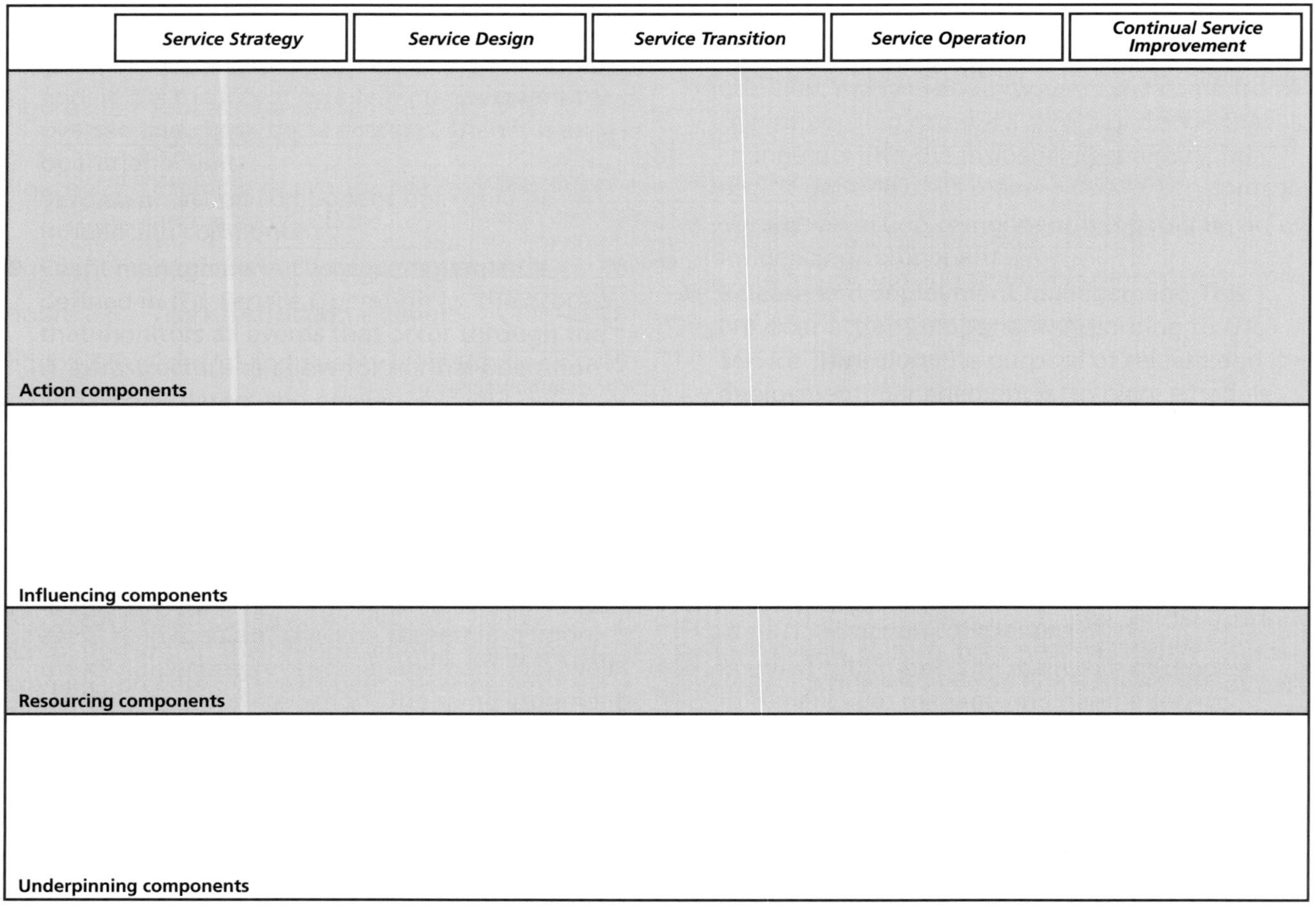

	Service Strategy	Service Design	Service Transition	Service Operation	Continual Service Improvement
Action components					
Influencing components					
Resourcing components					
Underpinning components					

Figure 5.2 Blank ITIL Lite master template

edition is represented in the template. Reading from top to bottom, you can see how each category is represented in the template.

Figure 3.8, the 'category to publication template', shows a version of this template with all of the ITIL components plotted onto it. You should have already decided on the categories for your components (see Chapter 3) and, using the template, it is a simple task to plot each component in the appropriate segment (as can be seen in the template examples that follow). Once you have entered your components, it's easy to see whether a well balanced approach has been chosen. This template can now guide the project into the implementation stage.

5.1 THE APPROACHES

The reasons for adopting ITIL Lite do not constitute a strategic approach. Each one of the reasons (see section 1.1) could have any number of potential strategic approaches. A strategic approach is how we undertake the selection of the components that will make up our ITIL Lite solution. Sections 5.1.1 to 5.1.12 describe some typical strategic approaches.

5.1.1 Bare necessities approach

This method is about including the barest of ITIL essentials. What constitutes these bare essentials would have ITIL wizards arguing for hours, because everyone will have their own idea about what is essential. However, the bare essentials are generally considered to be incident management, problem management, change management, service desk, and service asset and configuration management.

This would usually be seen as a first-phase approach but, if you have very limited resources, then it may be a good ITIL Lite approach. Incident, problem

and change management exist not only in every service management offering, but also in every IT department – even if it does not recognize service management as a discipline. The service desk also usually exists, but in the guise of a help desk. The key to success is to know which assets exist and how they are configured to provide a service. This is why service asset and configuration management has been included in the bare necessities approach, as shown in Figure 5.3.

The bare necessities template shows that the components are all based around the *ITIL Service Operation* and *ITIL Service Transition* publications and are concentrated in the action and influencing categories. The bare necessities provide an indispensable core for ITIL service management. When considering this approach, keep in the mind the following points:

- The lack of resourcing category components could lead to inefficiency and poor performance issues, especially as neither capacity nor availability management are present. Of course, it is possible that these functions are being performed elsewhere in your organization.
- Like the resourcing components, the underpinning category components may be covered elsewhere but, if outsourcers are being used, financial management and service portfolio management need to be considered to ensure that costs are managed. Similarly, service portfolio management can be used to ensure that the outsourcers are delivering the correct levels of service.
- Ignoring continual service improvement should not be too much of a problem if you fully implement the bare necessity components and apply them diligently, especially problem management and change management –

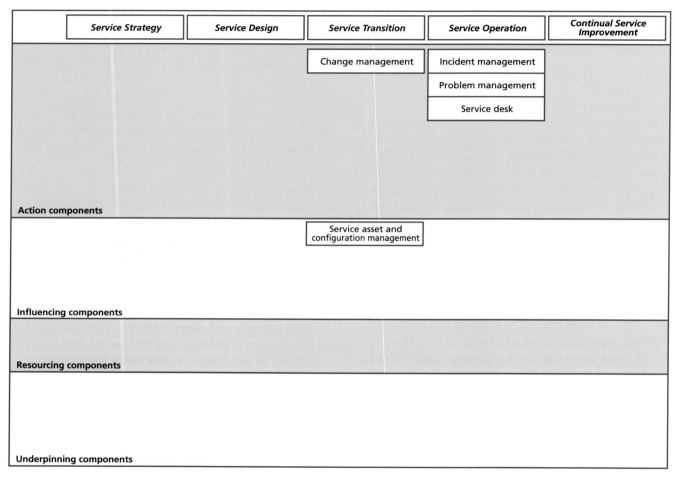

	Service Strategy	Service Design	Service Transition	Service Operation	Continual Service Improvement
Action components			Change management	Incident management	
				Problem management	
				Service desk	
Influencing components			Service asset and configuration management		
Resourcing components					
Underpinning components					

Figure 5.3 Bare necessities template

together these can dramatically improve the levels of service provided to IT service management customers.

- The *ITIL Service Strategy* and *ITIL Service Design* publications are there to ensure that new services arrive fully prepared to be quality accepted by service management. Not applying the processes in these publications can mean an excess number of incidents, problems and urgent change requests, particularly in the early days of a new system. Fully implementing change management will limit the damage, though. In change management, a request for change (RFC) should be submitted before work on a change is undertaken. This applies to new services as well as more traditional changes and allows a new service to be tracked through its development lifecycle. This is an important concession for change management, and one certainly worth pursuing.

■ You will get high returns on savings and efficiencies because these components represent what is often called 'low-hanging fruit'. Incident, problem and change management are relatively cheap and easy to implement, although service asset and configuration management can, unfortunately, be more expensive.

■ A help desk is probably already in place, so this is a low-cost item. Upgrading from a help desk to a service desk will improve the service to your customers.

■ The bare necessities will bring discipline and structure to service management which, in itself, is a huge advantage.

■ This approach tends to work best when you have no support from outside service management, and there are limited funds to implement ITIL. Although basic, this approach can be rewarding because, at completion, the very essence of service management will have been installed.

For many ITIL-inspired projects, it can be difficult deciding where to start but, with the bare necessities approach, the logical starting point is change management. If change management is controlled, you can use this to manage the implementation of other components, because they should commence with an RFC before any development work begins.

Bare necessities is as far as many organizations have progressed with their ITIL projects, because the returns have proven so valuable. The majority of organizations, however, will adopt a different approach.

5.1.2   Organic growth approach
The organic growth approach has been remarkably successful for some organizations. You begin by implementing just your essential components – as you would in the bare necessities approach. Once these have been implemented, you use the reporting from these to highlight the next component, or components, that need to be implemented. For example, if you find a lack of focus for your reports, you may decide to go on to implement service level management, or you may need to implement availability management because the service desk and incident management cannot restore service to the level demanded by your customers, as that level has not been established. The key to the success of an organic growth approach is to use the data from your existing processes to highlight the next component for your ITIL Lite project, and expand components into all categories.

5.1.3   Service support approach
Service support is easy to identify as a segment of ITIL v2 which concentrated on the basic process required to support customers and users on a daily basis. This is a simplified approach but can have great rewards if you are not already providing good support to your users and customers. The v2 version of service support consisted of the following functions and processes:

■ Incident management
■ Problem management
■ Change management
■ Release management
■ Configuration management
■ Service desk.

Even if this v2-oriented approach is chosen, the latest ITIL process or function should be used for the Lite project. There are some other significant ITIL processes and functions that should also be considered, including:

- Event management
- Request fulfilment
- IT operations management
- Service validation and testing
- Service catalogue management
- Service level management.

These are not necessarily recommendations, but suggestions that will give a much more rounded level of service support. Event management can link with incident management to provide cover for those incidents that affect service, or have a potential impact on service. Request fulfilment will take some of the pressure off change management while empowering the service desk to provide a more dynamic service to customers and users. The three service components will focus the other components to ensure that the levels of service provided by them meet the requirements of the customers.

If this approach is chosen, it is important to ensure that you use the latest ITIL equivalents to the v2 components, and identify those components that will strengthen and consolidate the service support components. You will find most of the processes that you need in *ITIL Service Operation* and *ITIL Service Transition*, as indicated in Figure 5.4.

Service support was the cornerstone of ITIL v2 and, as the template in Figure 5.4 illustrates, just like the bare necessities approach it focuses on *ITIL Service Transition* and *ITIL Service Operation* publications with just a hint of *ITIL Service Design*. However, you can see that it is a more expansive approach to

ITIL Lite than the bare necessities approach. Figure 5.4 contains two types of component – required components and additional components. The required components meet the service support criteria but fall short of a comprehensive service offering, because no service level data exists. But, when you add the additional components, it immediately becomes more rounded, encompassing three of the five publications.

This template would ensure full operational control of service management and, as a result, is a recommended approach for ITIL Lite, especially if the additional requirement components are included. There are some important points for consideration:

- Some of the components may already be in use, because of an earlier attempt at ITIL or because they are regarded as basic elements of IT (e.g. change management). If this is the case, ensure that you upgrade your components so that they are consistent with the latest ITIL guidance.
- A service support approach can be performance-oriented, which, in itself, can be very positive – although not if performance is achieved without quality of service levels being followed. This is why service catalogue and service level management have been included as additional components.
- You will get high returns on savings and efficiencies because these components represent what are often called 'low-hanging fruit'. In the case of incident, problem and change these are relatively easy and cheap to implement. Unfortunately, service asset and configuration management is more expensive.
- A help desk is probably already in place, so this is a low-cost item. Upgrading from a help desk to a service desk will improve service to customers.

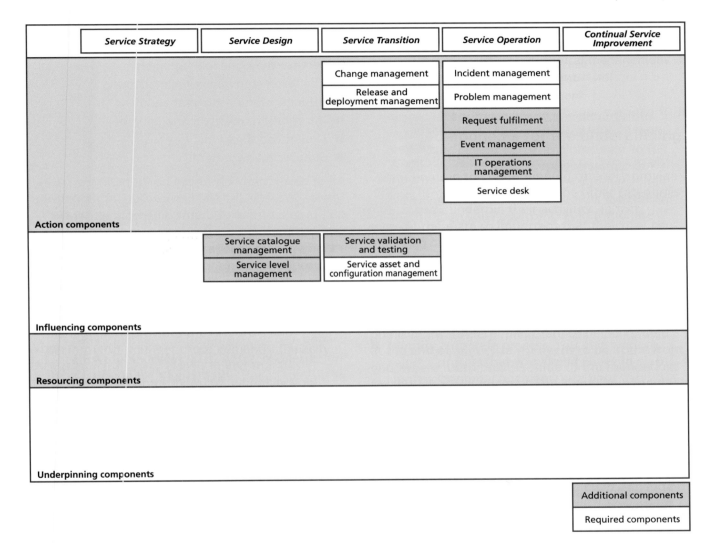

Figure 5.4 Service support template

- This approach will bring discipline and structure to service management and this, in itself, will be further enhanced if you include the additional components because they will focus your service management offering.

- *Service Support* was the most widely implemented v2 publication so it has a proven pedigree.

■ This approach tends to work best for ambitious service management organizations that have no support from outside service management, and have limited funds to fully implement the ITIL service lifecycle.

■ The service support approach can be implemented with little or no support from the customer, and only limited support from the rest of IT, if only the required components are included. If the additional components are included, then some support from the customer and IT will be required.

This approach is aimed at service support so, when adopting it, the required components should be implemented first, before proceeding to the additional components, bearing in mind that change management is still a good starting point. This is a very good approach for ITIL Lite.

5.1.4 Service delivery approach

Service Delivery is the other key publication from ITIL v2 and, generally, the same rules apply here as for the service support approach. However, it is hard to see how this approach could be successful without some of the components from service support being in place. The components in *Service Delivery* for service support are:

■ Financial management
■ Service level management
■ Capacity management
■ Availability management
■ IT service continuity.

If you decide to go down this v2-oriented approach ensure that you use the equivalent ITIL lifecycle processes or functions. There are some other significant ITIL processes and functions that are also worth considering, such as:

■ Demand management
■ Service portfolio management
■ Service catalogue management
■ The seven-step improvement process
■ Business relationship management
■ Information security management
■ Design coordination
■ Supplier management.

All of these components can be found in the *ITIL Service Strategy* and *ITIL Service Design* publications but, because none of them come from either *ITIL Service Operation* or *ITIL Service Transition* there is a distinct lack of action components (see Figure 5.5).

This is a rare approach because most organizations concentrate first and foremost on service support, especially those organizations that implemented ITIL v2. Sometimes IT service management is divided into two groups of components, with one group performing the operational tasks and the other performing the planning and customer communication functions. In this case, it makes sense to take this approach although it is dangerous to make claims (e.g. SLAs) without the operational services in place to deliver them.

This approach is interesting because it highlights how some of the old v2 components have been rationalized into two or more components:

■ Demand management used to be part of capacity management, and was used in conjunction with workload management
■ The service catalogue was a component under the area covered by service level management.

Those of us experienced in v2 will notice that there are two additional components with which we are not familiar: supplier management and service portfolio management, which are now

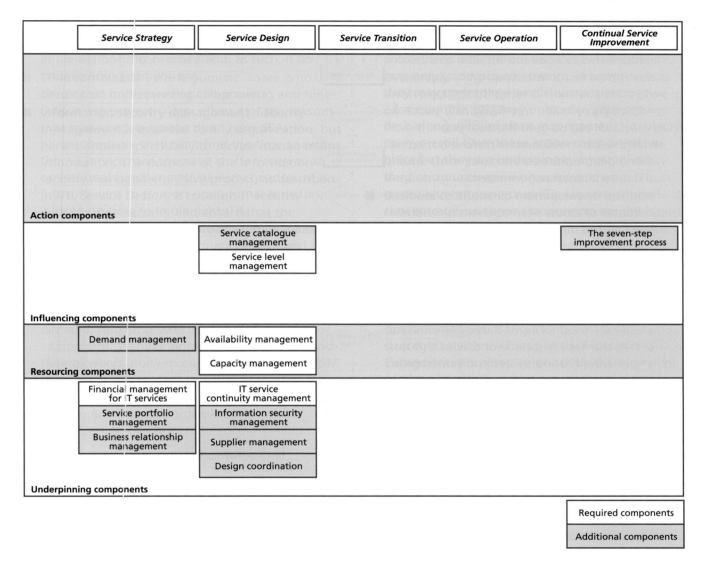

Service Strategy	Service Design	Service Transition	Service Operation	Continual Service Improvement

Action components

| | Service catalogue management | | | The seven-step improvement process |
| | Service level management | | | |

Influencing components

| Demand management | Availability management | | | |
| | Capacity management | | | |

Resourcing components

Financial management for IT services	IT service continuity management			
Service portfolio management	Information security management			
Business relationship management	Supplier management			
	Design coordination			

Underpinning components

| Required components |
| Additional components |

Figure 5.5 Service delivery template

significant components in ITIL. This indicates that those who have already implemented ITIL v2 just need to bring their existing components up to the standard defined in the latest guidance, and then

install supplier management and service portfolio management. Take into account the following points when deciding upon this approach:

■ Some components may already be in use from an earlier attempt at ITIL, or because they are regarded as basic elements of IT. If this is the case, these components should be upgraded so that they are consistent with the latest ITIL guidance.

■ A service delivery approach creates an environment in which service management can flourish. This is positive if the performance is not lacking because of poor delivery.

■ If there is a separate service support facility, then it is important to work in conjunction with it when implementing a service delivery approach to ensure that a united level of service is being provided to customers.

■ Implementing a service delivery approach will not give a fast return on investment because not many of the components can automatically build their services, e.g. a discovery tool will not deliver much of the data required for service delivery. Many of the deliverables will have to be created with large amounts of manual input, especially service level management, service catalogue management, service portfolio management and IT service continuity management. Once built, these services are then easy to maintain but the initial effort should not be underestimated.

■ Some of the components in service delivery are quite specialized – for example, capacity management, availability management and demand management all require specific technical skills, while financial management obviously requires accounting skills. These specialized skills make this approach more of a management function than a set of processes.

■ You probably already have financial management in place, so this would be a low-cost item to implement. The rest depend upon how far you progressed into v2.

■ This approach will bring deliverables to harness the rest of IT service management to stop them putting performance before quality.

■ Of the two most-implemented v2 publications (*Service Delivery* and *Service Support*), *Service Support* was more widely implemented than *Service Delivery*, although enough organizations did implement *Service Delivery* to prove its viability.

■ This approach tends to work best for service management organizations that work closely with their customers, rather than those that work closely with technicians.

■ The service delivery approach can only be successfully implemented with support from customers and the rest of IT.

What makes service delivery unique is that it can be owned by a non-IT group, even though it will involve IT technicians. For example, the settings of capacity thresholds and the measuring of these thresholds could be performed by customers, with IT technicians providing technical support when those thresholds are breached. It is not likely that many organizations will use this Lite approach but those that do will enjoy success if they maintain a close relationship with their customers during implementation.

5.1.5 V2 approach

To some extent, this is an amalgamation of the previous two approaches and is favoured by organizations that already have v2 in place and want to update it, rather than fully implement ITIL. If you decide to go down this v2-oriented approach you should use the equivalent process or function. Some of the processes need to be reconsidered because they have had some components extracted as separate components in the latest ITIL guidance. For example:

- Demand management was part of capacity management but is now a unique component.
- Service level management has been divided into service level management, service portfolio management and service catalogue management.
- Event management has been extracted from incident management to become a unique component.
- Request fulfilment has emerged from change management and the service desk.

There are some other components that have emerged, but these are the key ones to consider at a Lite level.

You will notice that service portfolio management has been added as an additional component (see Figure 5.6). This is to ensure that all of the other components concentrate on providing services in a common and structured manner. SLAs are important but, in order to create them, you have to understand the scope of the service. Therefore, it's important to consider service portfolio management in this approach.

V2 is a well-proven approach that has a long and successful pedigree and meets most of the criteria required to obtain ISO/IEC 20000 certification. Take into account the following points when considering this approach:

- If v2 has already been partially, or fully, implemented, then some of the components will already be in use. This will save time and speed up implementation.
- A gap analysis must be performed to differentiate between the components that you already have in place and the level defined in

the latest ITIL guidance. Gap analysis compares the current components with the ITIL versions to determine the workload and cost of bringing your v2 components up to the latest standard described.

- A v2 approach covers the fundamental and operational aspects of v2 but does not cover all of the aspects described in the *ITIL Service Design* and *ITIL Service Strategy* publications, so it could be a little reactive as a result. If this approach is adopted make sure that you get involved in projected services and systems as soon as possible and ensure that you can provide an environment for tomorrow as well as for today.
- As you can see from Figure 5.6, there are no components from *ITIL Continual Service Improvement*. If you adopt this approach care should be taken to ensure that the focus remains on maintaining levels of service and improving that service.
- The more of v2 already implemented, the more likely it is that you can achieve this approach quickly and cost-effectively (but don't forget that gap analysis!)
- This approach is a mixture of service and technical skills and often works better as part of a separate service management department, so that these diverse teams can be harnessed into a single focused unit.
- You probably already have financial management in place, so this should be a low-cost item to implement. The rest depends upon the extent to which v2 was implemented.
- This approach will give you the components required to obtain ISO/IEC 20000 certification and if information and security management, along

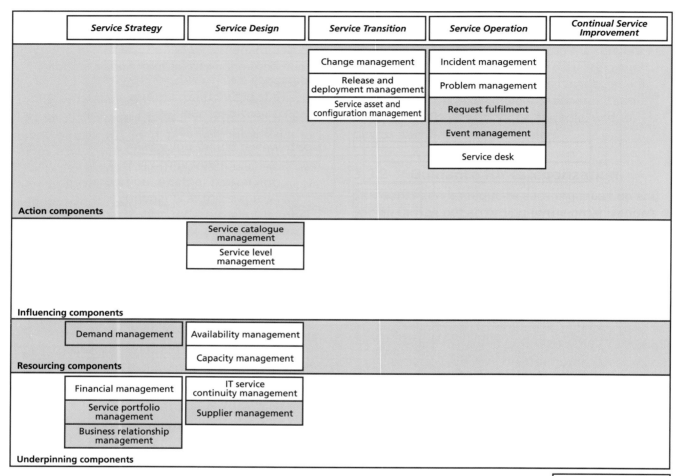

	Service Strategy	Service Design	Service Transition	Service Operation	Continual Service Improvement
			Change management	Incident management	
			Release and deployment management	Problem management	
			Service asset and configuration management	Request fulfilment	
				Event management	
				Service desk	
Action components					
		Service catalogue management			
		Service level management			
Influencing components					
	Demand management	Availability management			
		Capacity management			
Resourcing components					
	Financial management	IT service continuity management			
	Service portfolio management	Supplier management			
	Business relationship management				
Underpinning components					

Required components
Additional components

Figure 5.6 V2 template

with access management, is also included the organization will be in a good position to obtain ISO/IEC 20000.

- For many organizations, implementing v2 was problematic, but with this approach the difficulties will be limited because you should have learnt from your first experience, and the advantages and benefits of ITIL can be proven.

This is a tried-and-tested approach, updated to meet the demands of modern services, and it will provide great service and support. It can be controlled by service management with minimum dependency on other IT groups and teams.

5.1.6   V2 plus approach

If you already have v2 in place, but want to go just a little further to achieve your version of ITIL Lite, you will have to select the extra processes to supplement and improve the existing v2 components. The following components, along with the 11 v2 ones, would provide a great version of ITIL Lite:

■ Event management
■ Request fulfilment
■ Service catalogue management
■ Demand management
■ Service portfolio management
■ Service catalogue management
■ Supplier management.

It may have been decided not to implement all of v2, so it is a good idea to double-check any components that have already been rejected to see if they now need including in your Lite version. You should also check to see if any of the v2 processes need updating. V2 plus allows you to harness what has already been completed so far, with the added bonus of consolidating the service with some of the power processes from the latest ITIL guidance (see Figure 5.7).

You will notice that we have included the seven-step improvement process from the *ITIL Continual Service Improvement* publication in this template. This is to eliminate the greatest weakness of the v2 approach, which is that it focuses on fire-fighting rather than

fire prevention. Most of the points for consideration from the v2 approach apply here, but there are a few more to add:

■ This is a balanced and well-structured approach because it includes all five ITIL publications and all of the four categories.
■ Adding the CSI materials to v2 is a logical progression, especially for service management departments who are not involved in the development lifecycle.
■ Most of the data required by CSI is already being collated by the v2 components so, again, it is a logical fit.
■ This template works well for organizations that have already implemented all or part of ITIL v2, but it is more challenging for organizations starting with ITIL for the first time. In this case, it may be better to first implement a simpler approach, such as bare necessities or service support, and then progress on to this approach.

Although this approach is not a full lifecycle approach, it is well balanced and comprehensive and would provide an ideal Lite solution for most service organizations.

5.1.7   Lifecycle approach

ITIL is based on a lifecycle approach so it follows that a Lite approach could be based on the same principle. This approach makes good sense, particularly if you are intending to eventually progress to full ITIL implementation. For this approach, all five ITIL publications would be used as a guide to selecting the components.

As you can see from Figure 5.8 this is not likely to be a feather-light approach, but it clearly follows the lifecycle philosophy and would provide an ideal platform for the possibility of progressing to full

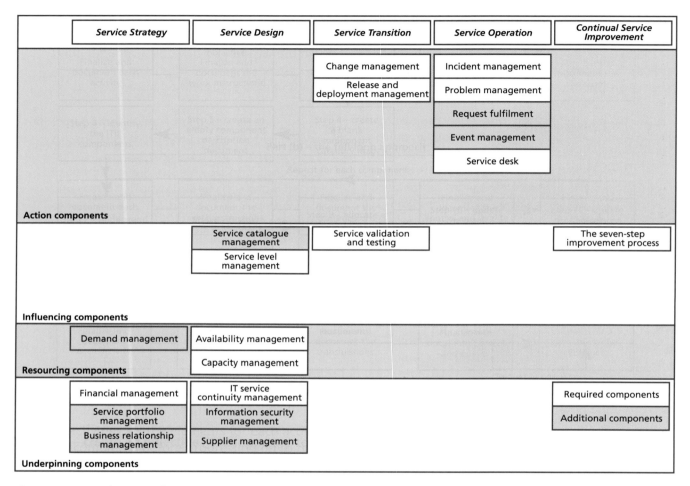

	Service Strategy	Service Design	Service Transition	Service Operation	Continual Service Improvement
Action components			Change management	Incident management	
			Release and deployment management	Problem management	
				Request fulfilment	
				Event management	
				Service desk	
Influencing components		Service catalogue management	Service validation and testing		The seven-step improvement process
		Service level management			
Resourcing components	Demand management	Availability management			
		Capacity management			
Underpinning components	Financial management	IT service continuity management			Required components
	Service portfolio management	Information security management			Additional components
	Business relationship management	Supplier management			

Figure 5.7 V2 plus template

ITIL implementation in the future. This approach is unique because it is more about which components to reject than which ones to include. Keep in mind the following points for consideration:

■ There is a good balance here because all five ITIL publications are included and all of the four categories represented, which gives both balance and structure.

■ This approach follows the lifecycle philosophy upon which ITIL is based.

■ It also includes CSI components, which means that it follows the Deming Cycle (seven-step improvement process), as well as the lifecycle structure.

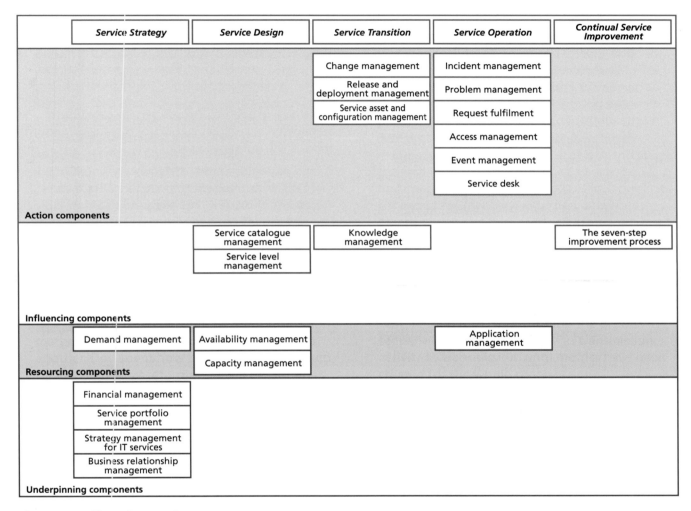

Service Strategy	Service Design	Service Transition	Service Operation	Continual Service Improvement
Action components		Change management	Incident management	
		Release and deployment management	Problem management	
		Service asset and configuration management	Request fulfilment	
			Access management	
			Event management	
			Service desk	
Influencing components	Service catalogue management	Knowledge management		The seven-step improvement process
	Service level management			
Resourcing components	Demand management	Availability management	Application management	
		Capacity management		
Underpinning components	Financial management			
	Service portfolio management			
	Strategy management for IT services			
	Business relationship management			

Figure 5.8 Lifecycle template

- Most of the data required by CSI is already being collated by the ITIL components so, again, CSI is a logical fit.
- IT operations management, technical management, service validation and testing, evaluation, and transition planning and support have all been omitted because they are often performed outside the control of service management.
- IT service continuity, information security management and supplier management have been omitted for similar reasons, but could be included if they are not performed elsewhere.

■ This template works well for organizations that have already implemented all, or part, of ITIL v2 but is more challenging for those starting with ITIL for the first time. In this case, it may be better to first implement a simpler approach, e.g. bare necessities or service support, before progressing to this approach.

Taking a lifecycle approach is admirable but it does require a lot of components before any level of success can be guaranteed. Some of the *ITIL Service Operation* components could be removed but this would reduce the amount of data available to CSI. Overall, this is an excellent approach but not one that can be implemented quickly.

5.1.8 Service improvement approach

This is a good approach for those who already have in place a good service management process and would like to add CSI because it focuses on process improvement rather than process implementation. If you are thinking of taking this approach make sure that you perform a gap analysis to assess how well current processes match up to the ITIL processes, and to check that your processes are sound and comprehensive. If you find any significant gaps you should close them before continuing with a service improvement approach. This approach is unique because it is aimed specifically at one publication, *ITIL Continual Service Improvement*, rather than a set of processes. To work successfully, CSI needs data (the more the better), in which case you will need to include in your approach processes such as:

■ Incident management
■ Event management
■ Change management
■ Problem management
■ Release and deployment management

■ Service desk
■ Service asset and configuration management
■ The seven-step improvement process.

These processes will provide vital data and feedback to fully support CSI (see Figure 5.9). It is also possible that you will need to include service catalogue management and service portfolio management to provide the deliverables for CSI.

You could argue that a CSI approach would require every other component to be in place for true success. After all, it is based around the Plan–Do–Check–Act method pioneered by Deming. Because time and money are not unlimited, this diluted approach has been designed to give the most success from limited amounts of these resources. If considering this approach, keep in mind the following:

■ For a few components there is a good balance here because all five ITIL publications have been included and three of the four categories are represented, which gives both balance and structure.
■ The approach follows the Plan–Do–Check–Act method, a policy upon which ITIL is based.
■ Most of the data required by CSI is already being collated by the other components so CSI is a logical fit.

This template works well for a group charged with implementing CSI, but it does not give a good overall balance for an ITIL Lite offering. Often, CSI is seen as the driving force of a second-phase stage of ITIL implementation.

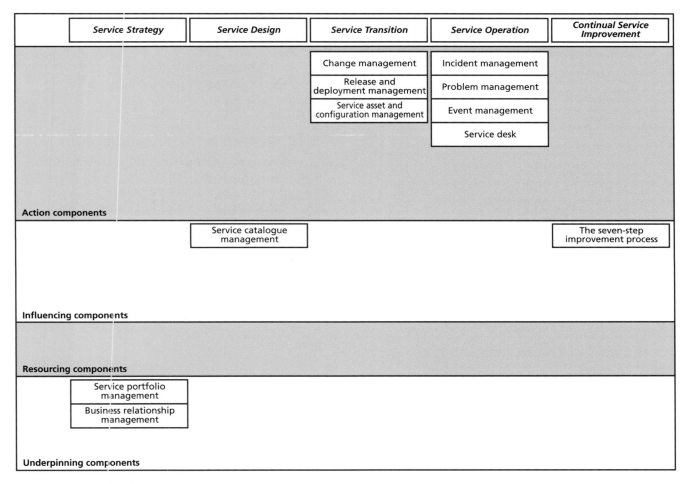

Service Strategy	Service Design	Service Transition	Service Operation	Continual Service Improvement
		Change management	Incident management	
		Release and deployment management	Problem management	
		Service asset and configuration management	Event management	
			Service desk	
Action components				
	Service catalogue management			The seven-step improvement process
Influencing components				
Resourcing components				
Service portfolio management				
Business relationship management				
Underpinning components				

Figure 5.9 Service improvement template

5.1.9 Service operation approach

This approach is fairly common, especially in large mainframe legacy sites where operation was, and still is, a driving force for providing customer services. In fact, many of the early help desks emerged from operational IT groups. Although not true to the purist ITIL edicts, this approach can have great effects and quickly because it concentrates on the action components (see section 3.2.1). This approach focuses on ensuring that the action processes are successfully in place and fully functional. In some organizations, the customer community is not interested in IT services and, for example, rejects SLAs, in which case this can be a good approach. Typically, processes that would be included in this approach are:

- Service desk
- Incident management
- Problem management
- Event management
- Change management
- Release and deployment management
- Request fulfilment
- IT operations management
- Access management
- Service asset and configuration management
- Application management
- Technical management.

Because this approach does not include any influencing components, it may be a good idea to consider adding service level management and service catalogue management to this list, to provide direction and targets. Figure 5.10 illustrates some potential components for this approach.

Service operation is key to the success of any ITIL implementation but here it is the final deliverable. Consider the following points if embarking on this approach:

- This approach has been based around the *ITIL Service Operation* publication but needs support from some of the other components for any real degree of success. In particular, it requires help from the service transition components: change management, release and deployment management, and service asset and configuration management.
- If the service operation approach is being carried out as part of a larger ITIL implementation, it is important to ensure that you regularly consult with other ITIL builders.

Focusing on one publication can cause problems, because the ITIL publications are designed to work as a cohesive unit. This is why it is recommended that, when adopting this approach, some components from other publications are also included.

5.1.10 Service ownership approach

This approach is based around those processes for which ownership exists. ITIL may not be a common goal and while some may be keen to adopt it, other IT groups that own some of the processes may refuse to participate. This should not be seen as a reason to abandon ITIL, but rather a reason to implement those processes for which you have ownership, and use your success to encourage other groups to implement their processes. The approach is straightforward – create a template that matches the services owned and remember the following points:

- This approach is based around the services that you own. Because you will already be familiar with the functionality of those services, making them ITIL conformant shouldn't be too tricky.
- The primary concern here is with the difference between how the existing components function and the ITIL definitions. Your main activity will be to perform a gap analysis to identify and resolve these differences.
- You may identify some other components that will affect your version of ITIL Lite. If so, discuss them and your plans with the owners of the other components.
- If components that do not exist within the organization are identified, then they should be added to the template as potential components.

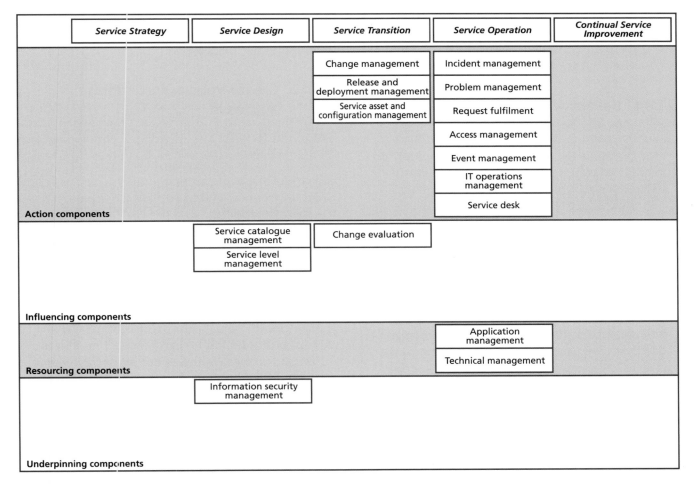

	Service Strategy	Service Design	Service Transition	Service Operation	Continual Service Improvement
Action components			Change management	Incident management	
			Release and deployment management	Problem management	
			Service asset and configuration management	Request fulfilment	
				Access management	
				Event management	
				IT operations management	
				Service desk	
Influencing components		Service catalogue management	Change evaluation		
		Service level management			
Resourcing components				Application management	
				Technical management	
Underpinning components		Information security management			

Figure 5.10 Service operation template

- Keep in mind that your changes may affect owners of the other components. So keep them informed of your actions.
- If the service ownership approach has been chosen because the ITIL Lite project is occurring as part of a larger ITIL implementation, then it's essential that you regularly consult with the other ITIL builders.

- For a small selection of components, this is a balanced and structured approach which represents all five ITIL publications and all four categories.
- Remember to create a balance between the publications and the categories.

Ensure that current processes function to ITIL standards before adopting any new processes. Any success with new processes can be used to encourage groups that may still be anti-ITIL.

5.1.11 Best-practice approach

If the primary objective is to implement another best practice or standard (such as COBIT, ISO/IEC 20000 or ISO/IEC 27001) and implementing ITIL is your secondary objective, then the project will be driven by the requirements of the other best practice. For example, it is possible to obtain ISO/IEC 20000 certification without having to implement all of the processes.

If you are looking to implement a Lite version of ITIL based upon another best practice, then guidance can be obtained from those best practices – for example, both ISO/IEC 20000 and COBIT are very closely related to ITIL. If in doubt, cross-reference ITIL with the best practice that you are adopting to identify the appropriate processes. Keep the following points for consideration in mind:

- It's important to learn about the best practices being utilized to ensure that the correct level of education for the appropriate staff is obtained.
- Check with the best practice to see if it has any templates or guidance that may help.
- When selecting components, do not reject other components without ensuring that they will not make a positive contribution to the project.
- When planning an ITIL Lite best-practice approach, it's always worth checking what the next release of ITIL will contain in order to stay ahead of the game, if that is possible.
- If some of the components are already in place, ensure that they are functioning to ITIL standards.

- Because ITIL Lite is part of a larger project, it's important to liaise closely with other teams working on the project.

5.1.12 Create-your-own-template approach

A number of templates have been suggested although it is difficult to provide one for every situation, and you may prefer to create your own. Having selected your components, you can now add them to your customized template, keeping in mind the following points:

- When creating your template remind yourself of why you are implementing ITIL Lite – because you will be measured against these reasons.
- It can be tempting to add too many components, so ensure that every component is essential because you will be expected to deliver all of the components present on the template. You could take a two-phase approach, and indicate the phase one and phase two components on your template.
- Creating a template should be a group activity and involve all staff.
- Make sure that you have a good balance between publications and components.

Creating your own template from scratch is both challenging and rewarding and, for many organizations, represents the best route to success. However, it relies heavily on a sound understanding of ITIL, so experience and education are integral.

All of the above approaches, including the customized template, are valid ways of initiating an ITIL Lite project. They are, however, just a guide and you may develop your own approach based upon individual needs and demands.

5.1.13 Classic ITIL Lite – a suggested start for adopting ITIL

As we have already seen, there are endless ways to structure the ITIL framework to meet your specific requirements. When starting on our ITIL journey, however, most of us need some help because there are often more questions than answers: 'Where should I start? What makes the best ITIL Lite framework? How many ITIL components should be included in ITIL Lite?' There is an old expression that says, 'Experience is something you get just *after* you needed it.' When you are building an ITIL framework you cannot afford mistakes, so the expression should read, 'Experience is something you get just *before* you need it.' That, in a nutshell, is what we shall explain; ITIL Lite is the result of experience and collaboration.

As you can see from Figure 5.11 there are six components in the classic ITIL Lite framework.

At first glance you are probably asking where component X is, and what happened to component Y? For example, what happened to configuration management? This is natural, because we all have our own interpretation. So why were these six components chosen? To explain this we need to look at the role of each classic component in detail:

■ **Service asset (and configuration) management**
Only service asset management has been included in the classic ITIL Lite template (see Figure 5.12) because managing assets is a basic responsibility for managers and staff in all organizations and enterprises. It is also extremely important for IT service management and ITIL. It is worth remembering that ITIL is an abbreviation of Information Technology Infrastructure Library, with infrastructure being a key element. Without asset management it is very difficult to

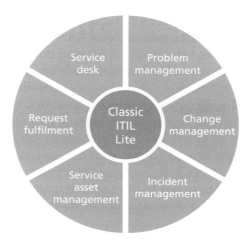

Figure 5.11 Classic ITIL Lite components

have a managed and controlled infrastructure. Installing and managing assets is a relatively straightforward activity that can be completed fairly quickly. Configuration management, on the other hand, is time-consuming and can delay adoption of the other classic components. Configuration management is a very important component of ITIL, though, and should be employed as soon as possible after the classic components have been adopted. Organizations without control of their assets may well be breaking governance regulations.

■ **Service desk** This is a classic component because all IT departments will get communications from their customers concerning errors or other issues that they may be having. It is vital that an effective and efficient service desk is established because the service desk is often seen as the 'face' of IT; a poor service desk suggests that IT is not competent, whereas an excellent service desk can engender a feeling that IT is efficient. In addition, the service desk collates vital data to help improve IT support and services.

- **Incident management** Communications with the service desk can be classed as either incidents or requests. The ITIL glossary states, 'incident management ensures that normal service operation is restored as quickly as possible and the business impact is minimized'. This is why incident management has been included as one of the classic components. Notice, though, that it does not mention eliminating the incident; this is a task for problem management.

- **Problem management** A prime responsibility of any department in an organization or enterprise is to provide a top-class service to its customers and associated departments. This will entail eliminating errors and other issues. Incident management gets the customer's services restored to agreed service levels, but it is problem management that is responsible for eliminating those incidents. Problem management is responsible for root cause analysis, where the root cause is the underlying or original cause of an incident or problem. Without problem management customers would be unhappy, the number of incidents would grow rather than shrink, and the service desk would be inundated. It is for these reasons that problem management has been included as a classic ITIL Lite component.

- **Request fulfilment** At first this may seem a strange inclusion in a classic ITIL Lite framework, but it is key to customer satisfaction. It is quite obvious: the more efficiently you handle customer requests the better your relationship with your customers will become. Also, the data collated from dealing with customer requests can be very valuable when planning for ITIL service strategy and ITIL service design. One

bonus is that in many cases you can use the same software for request fulfilment as for incident management and service desk.

- **Change management** Change management is the key component of classic ITIL Lite because if you do not have control of your changes you are sailing in dangerous waters. Poor change management can have serious consequences such as expensive outages. Without good change management, the risk of serious incidents is increased. Change management is chosen simply to avoid these kinds of situations.

There are other outstanding candidates for inclusion in the classic ITIL Lite template: release and deployment management, event management and, of course, configuration management. As cloud-based services increase in volume and adoption, so does the importance of release and deployment management, because the more sources that contribute towards the flexibility of the cloud, the more difficult it becomes. Event management, on the other hand, provides extra resource to prevent potential interruptions to service. These are all good potential components, but the idea is to keep ITIL Lite as 'lite' as possible so they could be seen as future supplements to ITIL Lite.

Not only do the six classic ITIL Lite components individually provide a great basis for ITIL, but their case becomes even stronger when they are viewed as a unit rather than six isolated components. This can be achieved by exploring their common traits:

- **Universal** Whether they realize it or not, every IT resource has these basic components. In the current IT world there will always be changes, problems and assets and so on; it is more a case of how well they are handled than whether they exist. If they are not handled well, IT will not be capable of providing a high-quality service to

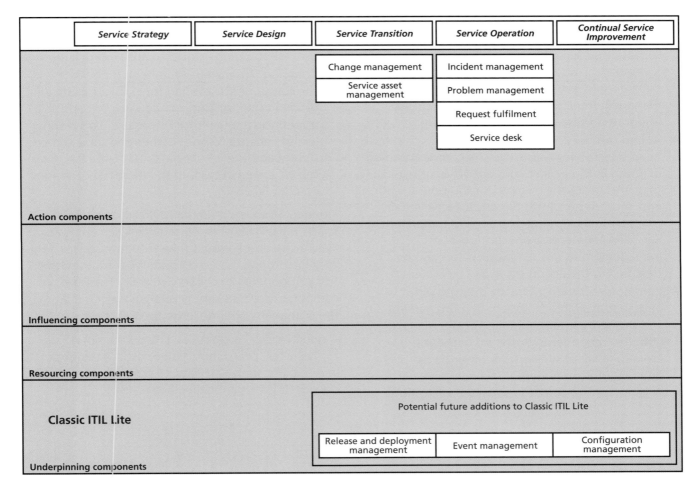

	Service Strategy	Service Design	Service Transition	Service Operation	Continual Service Improvement
			Change management	Incident management	
			Service asset management	Problem management	
				Request fulfilment	
				Service desk	
Action components					
Influencing components					
Resourcing components					
Classic ITIL Lite			Potential future additions to Classic ITIL Lite		
			Release and deployment management	Event management	Configuration management
Underpinning components					

Figure 5.12 Classic ITIL Lite template

its customers. Either way, they are omnipresent: wherever you find IT you will find these six components.

■ **Fundamental** What is the point of spending large amounts of time and revenue building and negotiating service level agreements with your customers if you cannot deliver the basic service requirements? This is not to say that service levels do not have a role to play at some time, but before discussing them with customers the basics of good service management must be in place. The six components selected as the classic version of ITIL Lite are simply fundamental to the success of IT service management.

- **Closely integrated** The six components are closely related to each other and, in some cases, so close that separating them can be difficult. Some organizations, for example, do not differentiate between incident and problem management. Figure 5.13 shows how closely integrated these classic components are.

- **Action category** All of the components that have been selected for classic ITIL Lite can be classified as being in the action category, which means that they are constantly changing, requiring attention and, most importantly, directly affect the daily processing. Because service asset management has been separated from configuration management in this template, it can also be classified in the action category.

- **Common software** Many of the software packages available from service management vendors will contain modules for the classic ITIL Lite components. Software packages are also likely to support the other three outstanding components. This is important because having common software will reduce software purchasing costs, speed up software implementation, accelerate process automation, provide common interfaces and improve metrics.

- **Common IT unit/department** In many cases the components selected for classic ITIL Lite will reside in the same unit or department and share a common management structure. This is very useful because responsibilities and tools can be shared and the whole classic ITIL Lite resource can be driven according to one set of common objectives.

Figure 5.13 shows a simple, stylized example that charts only the high-level activities. For example, regular feedback would flow from the service desk to the customer, based on updates from the other five components to the service desk. These classic components are so closely related that in real time they can seem like one large process.

A good reason to create an ITIL Lite template such as classic ITIL Lite is that it is impossible to adopt ITIL in one giant step. You have to start somewhere, and classic ITIL Lite is an ideal place to start.

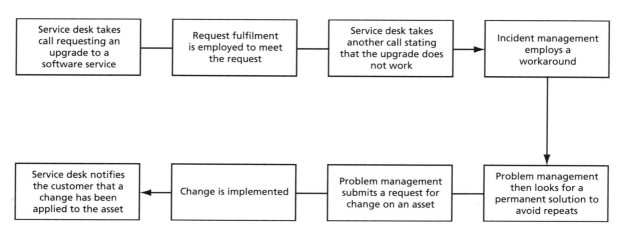

Figure 5.13 Relationships between classic components

5.2   CREATING AN ITIL LITE TEMPLATE

Now you have decided which approach to take, it's time to look at the steps required to build your template.

Figure 5.14 shows the steps required to create an ITIL Lite template. They are:

■ **Step 1 – review the reasons for adopting ITIL Lite**
It's important to review the reasons for choosing ITIL Lite (rather than full ITIL implementation) before creating a template, as the template must be designed to deliver those reasons.

You now need to decide whether you are going to utilize one of the templates provided in this publication or create a new one. Ideally, you would use one of the existing templates, customizing it to suit your individual needs. This would be quicker and easier than creating an entirely new one. It is possible, however, that after so much customization an existing template may resemble something entirely different. If a template fits the project then it should be used; if one doesn't then a new one will need to be created.

If you are going to use one of the templates in this publication, steps 2 and 3 should be completed as follows:

■ **Step 2 – select an ITIL Lite template** Keep in mind your reasons for building an ITIL Lite facility when you make this selection. The existing templates are just guides, and it is not necessary to select and comply completely with them. If one of the templates closely fits your requirements, then the decision is an easy one. Choose a template that fits the objectives of the project or, if this is not possible, match the filtered components with the templates.

■ **Step 3 – perform any component deletions**
Now that you have selected your template you need to look at all of the components in both the template and on your filtered list to ensure that they are relevant to the needs of the project, and delete any that aren't. It is most likely that components will be deleted from the supplied template, because your list of filtered components should not contain any unnecessary ones. A list of essential and potential components from the filtering process should remain in the template, ready for the final decision to be made in step 5. It's wise to use an obvious method for distinguishing the components (e.g. a colour code or a different shape for essential and potential) so that readers of the template can easily see what is going on.

If you are going to create your own template, steps 2 and 3 should be completed as follows:

■ **Step 2 – create a blank ITIL Lite template and decide upon a template theme** Use the blank template in Figure 5.2 as it is or customize it to meet your needs – for example, if you are going to use the v2 approach template there are no components from the *ITIL Continual Service Improvement* publication so you may want to remove this column.

Although it is not necessary, it makes sense to select a theme for your template by giving it a name (e.g. Business support). You could create your own theme or use one of the themes that we have described in this chapter, but with your own customization. Themes help because they focus attention. Just ask your service desk; they will have names for all their common incidents. The name should indicate the deliverables, just like the templates provided earlier in this chapter.

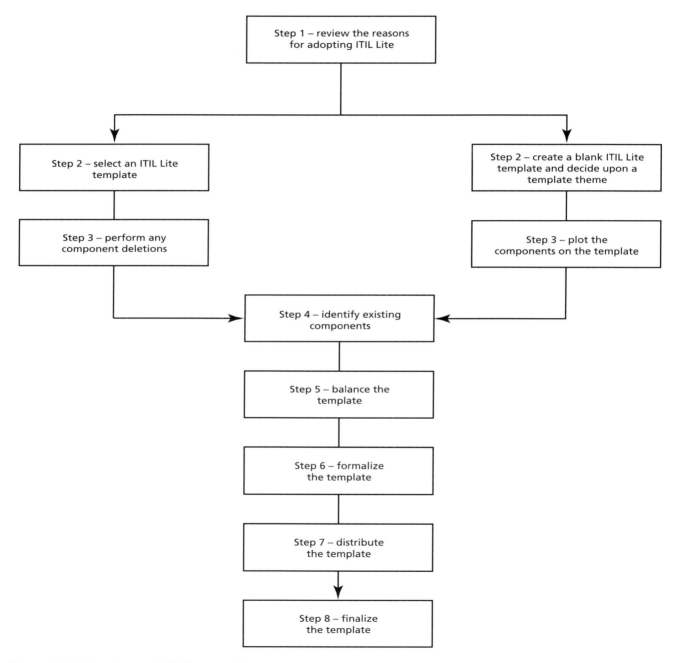

Figure 5.14 Creating an ITIL Lite template

■ **Step 3 – plot the components on the template**
There are two approaches that you can take
here: one is to use a blank template and plot
your components on it, the other is to create a
template with all the components on it, and then
delete any that do not apply. The latter option
is a good method because it ensures that you
haven't omitted any components that you may
require later.

**Whether you are using one of the published
templates, or creating your own, steps 4 to 8 will be
the same:**

■ **Step 4 – identify existing components** Update
your template with existing components – those
components that you already have in place.
You could use colours or shading to indicate
the difference between existing and additional
components. With the existing components in
place, your template will now give an indication
of the work required during implementation.

■ **Step 5 – balance the template** This is an
important task because you don't want an
unbalanced template – for example, too many
action components and not enough influencers,
or components all from one publication.

It's important to create a balance between the
components, and it may be worth reassessing
some of the rejected components at this stage.
Because this is not a full ITIL implementation,
not all of the categories and publications will
be represented. However, you should review
the categories and publications that are not
represented on your template to ensure that
you still have a good balance. Study the example
templates provided in this publication – few of
them will cover all the publications and all of the
categories. However, they are all well balanced
to meet the reasons for which they were created.

■ **Step 6 – formalize the template** This is the last
chance to double-check a template before it
is distributed to key IT personnel. Show the
template to all personnel who have been
involved or consulted during the project so far
and gather feedback. At this point, the template
becomes formalized.

■ **Step 7 – distribute the template** It is now time
for the template to be distributed to a wider
audience. There are several ways of doing this
but a face-to-face approach works best – this way
you know that the other person, or people, fully
understands the template and you can collate
their feedback immediately.

■ **Step 8 – finalize the template** Collate and
analyse the feedback. Depending upon the
comments, the template may need to be
amended, in which case it could be a good idea
to redistribute it. Either way you should now
produce the final version of your template.

The steps required to produce an ITIL Lite template
are quite straightforward and this can lead to
complacency. Follow the steps carefully; the success
of the ITIL Lite project rests on the production of
this template.

Preparing to implement ITIL Lite

6

6   Preparing to implement ITIL Lite

The template is now ready to be implemented. There is actually very little difference between implementing ITIL Lite and implementing full ITIL. In fact, the following points would need to be considered whether we were undertaking a full or a partial implementation:

- **Component maturity** It's essential, at this stage, to consider to what extent your components should be implemented. This is tricky, as service management differs from one organization to the next. There are tools – such as capability maturity modelling (CMM) and Capability Maturity Model Integration (CMMI) – that can be used to help you determine target levels of maturity. In the appendices of *ITIL Service Design* there is an ideal maturity model called the service management process maturity framework (PMF). Component maturity is an important subject because one of the most frequent mistakes is implementing ITIL components to the wrong level. This can be a waste of time, because a process is overimplemented or underimplemented and leaves some components ineffective. Ideally, you should determine the maturity level of all of the components in your ITIL Lite template.
- **Component priorities** We now need to consider the order in which the processes will be implemented. Component priorities are subjective and because every organization is different it follows that each plan will be

different too. The key is to understand what the most important components are for you and your organization.

- **Gap analysis** The objective of gap analysis is to determine the difference between the existing component and the equivalent ITIL component. This difference will help you to identify the cost, workload, tools, timing etc. required to implement that component.
- **Project management** ITIL Lite is a significant initiative (even if it is not as major as full ITIL implementation). To ensure success it is important that your ITIL Lite initiative is project managed and not an ad hoc activity without clear controls.

There may be other touch points between full implementation and an ITIL Lite project, but these are certainly the most prominent. Because there are so many processes, implementing any version of ITIL can be difficult and this is why planning is so important.

6.1   COMPONENT MATURITY

Now the template and its associated components are ready, the next step is to set the level, or maturity, of these components. We need to establish the level to which we want to implement each component before we perform a gap analysis. There are five levels in the process maturity framework. They are called maturity models because, as you progress from one level to the next, your component 'matures'. The five levels, as described in Appendix H of the *ITIL Service Design* publication, are:

■ **Level 1 – initial** The process has been recognized but there is little or no process management activity and it is allocated no importance, resources or focus within the organization. This level can also be described as 'ad hoc' or occasionally even 'chaotic'.
■ **Level 2 – repeatable** The process has been recognized and is allocated little importance, resource or focus within the operation. Generally activities related to the process are uncoordinated, irregular, without direction and are directed towards process effectiveness.
■ **Level 3 – defined** The process has been recognized and is documented but there is no formal agreement, acceptance or recognition of its role within the IT operation as a whole. However, the process has a process owner, formal objectives and targets with allocated resources, and is focused on the efficiency as well as the effectiveness of the process. Reports and results are stored for future reference.
■ **Level 4 – managed** The process has been fully recognized and accepted throughout IT. It is service-focused and has objectives and targets that are based on business objectives and goals. The process is fully defined, managed and has become proactive, with documented, established interfaces and dependencies with other IT processes.
■ **Level 5 – optimizing** The process has now been fully recognized and has strategic objectives and goals aligned with overall strategic business and IT goals. These have now become 'institutionalized' as part of the everyday activity for everyone involved with the process.

Other frameworks and maturity modelling approaches can be taken (e.g. CMM, CMMI) but we have chosen PMF because it is part of the ITIL family.

Later we will use gap analysis to identify the difference between your target PMF ratings and your actual PMF ratings (see section 6.4) – with the difference being the workload required to implement your template components. But, firstly, we need to decide upon the target maturity levels for our template components.

The eight steps for creating PMF maturity targets, as outlined in Figure 6.1, are:

1 **Select the maturity model** There are numerous maturity model frameworks, including CMM, CMMI and PMF. The most obvious choice is PMF because it is part of ITIL, but you can decide which framework best meets your needs. There is also the possibility that your organization is already using a maturity model framework, in which case you should consider adopting this standard framework because you will find expertise available and a level of creditability and acceptance of the framework already in place.
2 **Review the maturity levels** Review the maturity model framework in order to understand how it works. The definitions for each of the maturity levels need to be clearly understood, and any maturity levels that are not fit for purpose or do not apply should be noted.
3 **Amend the maturity levels if necessary** If in the previous step you identified any maturity levels that were not fit for purpose then you should amend them as necessary (remembering to check with all those involved in your ITIL Lite project).
4 **Select a template component** Because each component will be graded individually, it does not matter which component is selected first.

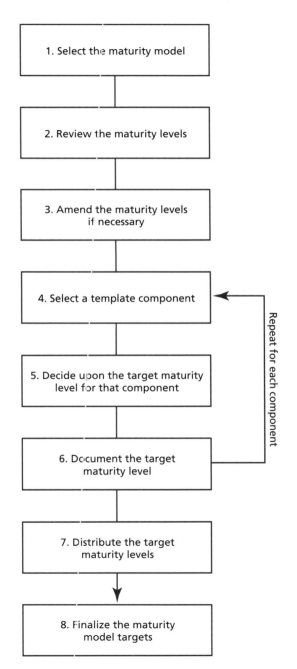

Figure 6.1 Creating PMF maturity targets

5 **Decide upon the target maturity level for that component** Decide upon the target level for the component selected in step 4. It is not necessary to have all component maturity target levels at the highest maturity level. Table 6.1 shows an example of some target maturity levels, using the service support template as a model.

Table 6.1 shows that change management has a target level of 5, while event management has a target level of 3 (remember these are just examples and not recommendations). It is critical that change management is at the optimized target level, as it must 'become 'institutionalized' as part of the everyday activity for everyone involved with the process' (*ITIL Service Design*). Because change will affect everyone at some time, then it logically follows that it would be at the highest maturity level. On the other hand, event management is typically contained within IT and fits nicely at the defined target level which states that 'the process has a process owner, formal objectives and targets with allocated resources, and is focused on the efficiency as well as the effectiveness of the process' (*ITIL Service Design*).

As a general rule, the higher the target level, the longer it takes to meet it and the more expensive it becomes. Therefore, it does not pay dividends to select a higher target level than is necessary. In Table 6.1 you can see that the lowest maturity level is a level 3. This is because it is the lowest maturity level with a process owner and, for many components (especially those that stay internal to IT), this is sufficient. Only you can decide on your target levels, based upon the maturity model framework you choose.

Table 6.1 Example target PMF level ratings

Template components	Target PMF level
Service desk	5
Event management	3
Incident management	4
Change management	5
Problem management	3
Release and deployment management	5
Service asset and configuration management	5
Request management	3
IT operations management	4
Service level management	5
Service catalogue management	4
Service validation and testing	3

6   **Document the target maturity level** Huge amounts of documentation are not necessary at this stage but it is important to document your reasons for selecting your target maturity levels. A simple spreadsheet, such as the one in Figure 6.2, allows all the selections to be seen at a glance.

7   **Distribute the target maturity levels** Now is the time to distribute your documentation and await feedback. You must decide how to perform the distribution – as a report, a presentation, or a one-to-one visit. Whatever method you choose, feedback should encouraged.

8   **Finalize the maturity model targets** Once all the feedback has been considered, and any appropriate action taken, you should finalize the maturity model targets and prepare for implementation.

Creating component maturity target levels is an interesting task and, because you have to look at the scope of each component in detail, can be a great learning exercise. The template and maturity model is now in place and the next step is to identify how much effort will be required to convert the current components to the target levels or, indeed, to implement missing components to the correct maturity level.

6.2   COMPONENT PRIORITIES

Careful consideration must be given to the order in which the ITIL Lite components will be implemented, so that you can gain maximum benefit as soon as possible while simultaneously maintaining control of your project. The objective here is to decide the order in which you will implement the components. There are different methods you can use to prioritize and schedule the implementation of your components:

■   **Quick wins (low-hanging fruit)** This is an obvious and traditionally popular approach in which those processes that can be implemented quickly are scheduled at the beginning of the project. The idea is that early successes will add credibility to the project and act as a stimulus to the team working on it. The downside is that these components may not be productive and may delay more productive and urgent components. For example, you may have poor, or no, change management but delay working on it in order to improve an already

	Change management	Incident management	Service desk
Level 5 -- OPTIMIZING		Other components ➡	
The process has now been fully recognized and has strategic objectives and goals aligned with overall strategic business and IT goals. These have now become 'institutionalized' as part of the everyday activity for everyone involved with the process. A self-contained continual process of improvement is established as part of the process, which is now developing a pre-emptive capability.	Description of the reason why this target level was chosen		Description of the reason why this target level was chosen
Level 4 – MANAGED			
The process has been fully recognized and accepted throughout IT. It is service focused and has objectives and targets that are based on business objectives and goals. The process is fully defined, managed and has become proactive, with documented, established interfaces and dependencies with other IT processes.		Description of the reason why this target level was chosen	
Level 3 – DEFINED			
The process has been recognized and is documented but there is no formal agreement, acceptance or recognition of its role within the IT operation as a whole. However, the process has a process owner, formal objectives and targets with allocated resources, and is focused on the efficiency as well as the effectiveness of the process. Reports and results are stored for future reference.			
Other levels ⬇			

Figure 6.2 Example of target maturity level documentation (descriptions taken from ITIL Service Design)

excellent incident management component. If you take this approach check that you are not jeopardizing any key components that need to be implemented urgently.

■ **Already in place** This is a variation on the 'quick wins' approach, except that it focuses on components that are, to some degree, already in place and leaves until last any components that need implementing from scratch. The same arguments and guidance explained in 'quick wins' also apply here.

■ **Maturity levels** We must now look at how the maturity levels described in section 6.1 can be used to create a schedule for the implementation of components. This can be approached in two different ways – implementing the highest target

maturity levels first or, conversely, implementing the lowest target maturity levels first. Either way, this is not ideal, as it's better to benefit from those components that have the most productive effect on your service management offering as soon as possible. This is an arbitrary approach, not much better than implementing components in alphabetical order. If you do adopt this approach you will need to perform a gap analysis first so that you know the difference between where you are and where you want to be, which will enable you to use maturity levels as an implementation plan.

■ **Already have existing technology** This approach has some real validity, especially if the technology applies to some significant components. Service management software is often built and sold as a package – for example, incident, problem, change and configuration management all bundled into one package. If we had only implemented incident and change, we may now elect to implement problem and configuration management before we progress to the other components in our template. This makes sense but only as a place to begin – you will still need to prioritize the rest of your components. This approach is similar, in many ways, to a quick-win approach.

■ **Risk boundaries** This is another selective approach and one that concentrates on prioritizing components depending upon the risk factor of each one. A typical method would involve starting with the low-risk impact components and graduating to the higher-risk impact components. This method would be adopted in the following way:

● Decide upon the parameters for your risk boundary, for example impact on the business, and a value to measure that impact, e.g. 1 for low-risk and 9 for high-risk. You could create a risk factor by adding a probability rating which would determine the potential for the respective components to fail. Again, a 1 to 9 rating would work, this time 1 being very unlikely to fail and 9 being most likely to fail. This would give you an impact probability (I:P) rating to help you more accurately prioritize your components. Only you can decide your risk factors.

● Identify a risk level for each component (I:P).

● Decide whether you will be implementing the high-risk components or the low-risk components first. Typically you would start with the lower-risk items so that you learn from your mistakes with minimum impact.

● You can now put your components into the order in which they will be implemented. Remember, the components you are prioritizing should be those that you have included in your template.

As a final check you may want to confirm the dependency of your components so that you are not trying to implement components that are dependent upon each other in the wrong order. Although this method has the advantage of lower risks, it will take much longer to reap the benefits from the project.

■ **Comfort factor** This method has a very similar structure to risk boundaries, with the exception that familiarity is used as a trigger. The concept is to install the components in an order based on how familiar those implementing them are with each component. For example, if you already have incident management in place you may decide to start here because you are familiar with the component and are comfortable working with it. A similar strategy to the one described in the risk boundaries method can be used here. There is one drawback, though – it is unlikely that you will be familiar with all of the methods. Therefore, you will still need to find a method to prioritize these components. If this is the case, then priority analysis or the interrelationships methods are recommended.

■ **Interrelationships** This is a more abstract approach where you review all of the components in your template to explore and consider their interrelationships and dependencies. For example, to stay accurate, service asset and configuration management requires that change management is in place. So, if you adopt this method you should implement change management before service asset and configuration management. Likewise, to be fully functional, problem management requires that incident management is in place, as this is the source for most of the data to identify new problems as they arise. Therefore, incident management is most likely to be implemented before problem management. To follow this method:

● Identify all of the components on the template.

● Identify a method to define the different types of relationships. You could use the relationship guidance from service asset and configuration management as a guide. The relationships are described in *ITIL Service Transition* as part of the service asset and configuration management section. Here are the same relationships, customized for this purpose:

    – A component is part of another component: this could occur when two components are very close – for example, you may decide that demand management should be integrated as part of capacity management.

    – A component is connected to another component: in this case, the components are closely coupled but still separate components – for example, change management coupled with release and deployment management.

    – A component uses another component: in this case, one component uses part of another component to fulfil its requirements – for example, incident management uses part of the contents of an SLA in service catalogue management to determine priority and escalation rules.

    – A component is installed at another location: this is because the ownership of a component is not within the implementation scope – for example, IT operations management is under a different management structure to IT service management, in which case these components need to be discussed with their respective owners to establish the interrelationships.

An organization can, of course, use its own relationship definitions, but you must identify a method of differentiating between the components:

● Take each component from your template and compare it with every other component from your template and note their relationships.

● From this data, prepare the order in which you will implement your processes.

When preparing your implementation plan, you may group some of the components together to form one implementation cluster, but the most important decision you will have to make is which components to start with. Typically, this would be the components with the most interrelationships with the other components, but you must also take into account the impact that the components can have on each other.

■ **Priority analysis** The objective here is to create a priority ratio and use this as the basis for prioritizing the components on your template. This gives a more balanced approach and allows everyone to clearly see the logic behind an implementation plan. A value to expenditure ratio (V:E) is a premier method for prioritizing template components:

● **Value** This is the value that the component has in relation to meeting the business requirements. This could be represented by a range of 1 to 9, with 9 being the maximum value. This would be the prime item in the ratio.

● **Expenditure** This is the extent of the expenditure that each component will have on the business when it is implemented. Expenditure will include cost of technologies and cost of effort required. This could be represented by a range of 1 to 9, with 9 being minimum expenditure. Component maturity and gap analysis will help you to calculate your expenditure.

To put this in perspective, here are some example V:E ratios:

● 9:9 means that this component has a high value to the business and low expenditure. This is a good ratio because it has high impact and low cost. Logically, this would be the first component to be implemented, unless there are some other 9:9 ratios.

● 1:1 means that this component has a low value to the business and a high expenditure. This is a poor ratio and therefore would be one of the last components to be implemented.

If you allocate a V:E ratio to all your template components you will be in a position to decide in which order you want to implement them. An easy way of doing this is to create a spreadsheet, like the one in Figure 6.3, which can then sort and produce a graphical illustration of the components and illustrate how they relate to each other.

Using the service support template, Figure 6.3 shows V:E ratio ratings and a quadrant graph illustrating their relationships. It's clear to see the priority order in the table. The chart not only reflects this priority order but also illustrates the relative importance of each component. The 'maximum value' and 'minimum expenditure' columns represent the V:E ratio. It is easy to cross-reference the chart and table because the values against the plot points in the chart refer to an item in the table – for example, the plot point 7,4 relates to service asset and configuration management because its table entries (V:E) are 7 and 4. There are four quadrants on the graph:

● **Quadrant A** This quadrant shows that you will obtain the maximum value with the minimum expenditure, so all the components in this quadrant are top of the priority list.

● **Quadrant B** The components in this quadrant have a high value to the business but require higher levels of expenditure. Components in this quadrant are likely to be completed next.

● **Quadrant C** Here we have low expenditure but also low value to the business. These components will be implemented ahead of the quadrant D components.

● **Quadrant D** Finally, quadrant D shows high expenditure and low value to the business, so it follows that these will be the last components to be implemented.

Remember, all the components will be included in your implementation plan because they are in your template – even the quadrant D components will be implemented. The components should now be in V:E priority order, but you may want to make some adjustments before you finalize your implementation plan list. In the example, change management was rated as 9:6, which means that it had a high

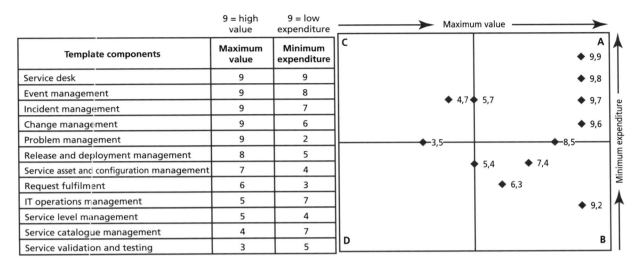

Template components	Maximum value	Minimum expenditure
	9 = high value	9 = low expenditure
Service desk	9	9
Event management	9	8
Incident management	9	7
Change management	9	6
Problem management	9	2
Release and deployment management	8	5
Service asset and configuration management	7	4
Request fulfilment	6	3
IT operations management	5	7
Service level management	5	4
Service catalogue management	4	7
Service validation and testing	3	5

Figure 6.3 A V:E quadrant graph

business value but required some investment, whereas event management also had a high business value but required less investment. Looking at the other merits of the components you may decide to change the order of your components to move change management up the list.

The methods described here are just a guide. Even if there is a favoured method, the essence of another method could still be used to help you make your final decision. For example, you may use the priority analysis method to create your original list, but the interrelationship method to finalize this list so that you implement dependent components correctly.

Component prioritization is only a seven-step plan (see Figure 6.4), but it's important in ensuring that the components are implemented in exactly the correct order:

1 **Select a method** Select the main method that will be used to establish the component priority order (CPO). Some methods (including quick wins, already in place, maturity levels etc.) have already been suggested, but you may wish to use your own.

2 **Create the method criteria** Whichever method you chose you will need to create some criteria or guidelines to provide the parameters for selection. For example, if you adopt the priority analysis method, a priority ratio needs to be created and described (a V:E ratio is recommended).

3 **Apply the method** This is the fun step! Apply your selected method to all of the components on your template. You may question your chosen method or you may question your criteria, but either way you must complete this step with your CPO in place before you can move on to the next step.

4 **Apply the essence of other methods** This step only occurs if you feel that you can improve your CPO by applying another method to your order. If this is the case, then you should select the method, create some criteria and apply it to your CPO order before continuing to the next step.

5 **Document the ITIL Lite component priority order** It is now time to begin the final stages by documenting your CPO along with all supporting data, such as graphs, maturity level ratings and gap analysis results.

6 **Distribute the ITIL Lite component priority order** This step can be performed in a number of ways (a report, a presentation, a one-to-one visit) but it is essential that feedback is encouraged – this is the last chance before the components are implemented.

7 **Finalize the ITIL Lite component priority order** Once you have collected feedback and taken any necessary action, finalize your CPO and prepare for implementation.

6.3 COMPONENT ACTION PLAN

A component action plan (see Figure 6.5) is a way to control and manage the work required for each of the components so that you can see at a glance the status of all the tasks pertaining to a component.

The component action plan consists of the following:

■ **Component** Enter the name of the component that will be controlled by this form/spreadsheet, e.g. service desk or change management.

■ **Owner** This is the owner of the work, and not the master action plan manager (although it is possible that the master action plan manager could also own some of the component action plans). The component action plan owner is

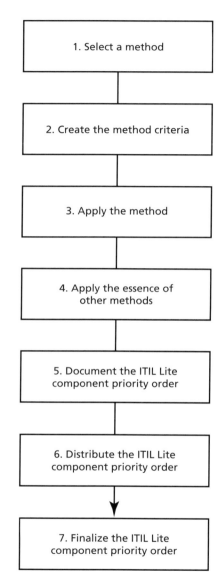

Figure 6.4 Component prioritization

ITIL Lite component action plan

Component _____   Owner_____

Category_____   Target maturity level _____ Actual maturity level _____ Target start date _____ Actual start date_____

Version number _____   Version date _____   Target end date _____ Actual end date _____

Ref. no	Defect	Action	Workload	Expenditure	Start date	End date	Analyst	Cross reference

More defects and actions

Figure 6.5 Component action plan

responsible for managing all of the actions listed in the plan for the designated component. This person is also responsible for updating the plan and feeding the results back to the master action plan manager.

■ **Category** In section 3.2 we identified four categories – action, influencing, resourcing and underpinning. Put the initial of the category you gave your component in this column. Both our components, service desk and event management, were given a category rating of A.

■ **Target maturity level** This is the target maturity level that was allocated during the component maturity stage.

■ **Actual maturity level** This is the actual maturity level that was allocated during the component maturity stage.

■ **Target start date** The target start date of the work for this component. This date should coincide with the start of work on the first action.

- **Actual start date** Ideally, this should be the same as the target start date. If it is earlier, that's not a problem, but if it is later, then you are already behind schedule.
- **Target end date** The date by which you plan to finish the actions required to complete the work on this component.
- **Actual end date** The actual date that you completed the work on this component and, ideally, the same as the target end date.
- **Version number** You will be required to update your component action plan at regular intervals. Each time you update the action plan, enter a version number here and forward on to the owner of the plan.
- **Version date** The date that this version of the component action plan was created.
- **Reference number** A unique reference number should be allocated for each defect that has been identified.
- **Defect** Include here a description of a defect that needs to be resolved. Every defect should have a separate entry along with a unique reference number. Typically, these defects would be identified in a gap analysis (see section 6.4). A defect is a fault or problem that needs to be resolved for this component to meet the required target maturity level. Typical resolutions include creating a process, installing monitoring, documenting work instructions, integrating two processes, identifying quality check points etc. If you are not using maturity modelling this would be a fault or problem that needs to be resolved in order for component implementation requirements to be met.
- **Action** Enter a brief description of the action that is to be taken to resolve the defect.

- **Workload** This is the estimated amount of work hours required to complete all of the actions necessary to remove a defect and improve the maturity level. By totalling this column you would be able see the number of estimated work hours required to complete the whole component action plan. An additional column could be added here with the actual number of hours worked so far on a component.
- **Expenditure** This column represents the estimated total expenditure for each action required to remove a defect and should include any technology purchases (plus their implementation costs), workload, consultants and training etc. By totalling this column, you would be able see the amount of estimated expenditure that needs to be spent to complete this action. You could also add an extra column here detailing the actual expenditure. This would enable a comparison of the actual expenditure with the allocated expenditure and means that expenditure on this component action plan can be controlled and reviewed. If the expenditure is updated regularly, this could then be entered into the master action plan to provide an overall status indication of the ITIL Lite project.
- **Start date** The date when work started on this defect. Two columns could be created here – target start date and actual start date – and, as a result, you would be able to monitor the progress of this action.
- **End date** The date when work was completed on this defect. Again, two columns could be created here – target end date and actual end date – to enable the progress of this action to be more closely monitored.
- **Analyst** The name of the person who is responsible for completing the actions.

- **Cross-reference** This refers to an associated process or activity, e.g. change reference number, project code, incident reference number etc. If you enter a value here then a reader can go to the reference point for more information. It is possible that some of the defects (e.g. creating a process from scratch) are stand-alone projects, in which case this information is invaluable.
- **More defects and actions** The example in Figure 6.5 only has space for three defects but, of course, you will require many more rows to enter all of the defects that you will need to resolve for a component.

You will need to use a computerized method (such as a spreadsheet, word processor or more specific product) to create your component action plan. A spreadsheet workbook is a good idea, where each sheet in the workbook is a different component. This allows you to store the status of all component action plans in one location.

The component action plans need to be created in anticipation of the gap analysis (see section 6.4). In a gap analysis, you will enter the defects and all other data into this form/spreadsheet to help you control the implementation. The spreadsheet is easy to create:

- **Decide upon the resource for your component action plan** A computerized resource is the best way to construct one. Unless specialized technologies are available, a spreadsheet is an inexpensive method.
- **Decide upon the contents of the component action plan** We have given an example of a component action plan layout, and suggested some ideas for extra columns that could make a component action plan more efficient. Decide

upon the contents of your action plan and get advice from experienced colleagues, such as project managers, if necessary.
- **Design your component action plan** When designing your component action plan keep in mind the ability to total columns and rows. If you are using a spreadsheet do not use the first page of the workbook because this is where the master action plan will go (see section 6.5).
- **Distribute your component action plan** Before finalizing your component action plan, distribute it and proactively obtain feedback to help improve the contents and layout.
- **Finalize the component action plan** Gather all of the feedback and finalize the layout and structure of your component action plan.

6.4 GAP ANALYSIS

Gap analysis is simple in theory, but it can be difficult and time-consuming to complete. In essence, gap analysis is intended to identify the difference between the target maturity level and the actual maturity level of a component, and then calculate the cost and effort required to close that gap.

There are only nine steps in a gap analysis closure plan, but they are all important and can mean the difference between success and failure for an ITIL Lite project. Don't forget to repeat each step for every template component:

- **Select a template component** Select your template components for gap analysis in CPO. If you have flexibility try and select a component that will have an actual maturity level close to the target maturity level. Start with components with small gaps, particularly if you have never performed a gap analysis before. This way mistakes can be easily rectified and you can perfect your skills on the easier tasks.

■ **Review target maturity level** This step should not take long; you are just familiarizing yourself with the target maturity level of the template component that you are working on. It is also the last logical point that you can challenge the validity of the allocated target maturity level. If you do challenge the target maturity level this is the time to discuss it with the relevant parties before continuing on to the next step.

■ **Determine actual component maturity level** You will need to look in detail at the template component you are working on and carefully compare the component with each level of the process maturity framework (PMF), or whichever maturity modelling approach you have selected. Start at the lowest level and progress upwards so, in the case of the PMF method, start at 1 and work upwards until you find the actual maturity level for the selected component. Document the actual maturity level and the reasons for your selection. If the component does not currently exist then you would automatically allocate a level 1 initial value. In fact, some maturity models have a 0 level called absence, or something similar. If this helps, you could add a 0 absence level to your maturity model.

■ **Distribute your actual component maturity level** Carry out a precautionary check to ensure that the correct actual maturity level for your component has been determined. Distribute and discuss the actual maturity level with the appropriate people within your organization. If they agree with your assessment you can proceed, but if they do not agree you will need to work with them until you come to an agreement. A key person to talk to is the owner

of the current component – for example, if you are working on incident management and this component is owned by the service desk manager then you must consult with this person before continuing. Some graphics may help you to illustrate your results at this point (see Figure 6.6).

■ **Identify the differences between target and actual levels** If your actual maturity level is lower than the target maturity level then you will need to identify those differences now so that the desired actual maturity level can be calculated. This can be a time-consuming task. This step is not looking at solutions, but at the drivers for solutions.

■ **Prepare a component action plan** Do not calculate expenditure or workloads at this stage; instead focus on building a plan that includes all the defect actions required to close the gap between the actual maturity and target maturity level. The only exceptions are those components that meet or exceed their target maturity level. There may still be one or two areas for improvement that need addressing. If so, create a plan for fine-tuning those components that require it. You could use a project management approach and produce a project for each template component. This is a particularly good idea if your organization is already using a project management methodology such as PRINCE2®.

■ **Calculate component action plan costs** Having prepared your plan, you can now calculate what it will cost to action it. These costs should include all of the data required to produce a budget for the plan:

Template components	Target PMF level	Actual PMF level
Service desk	5	4
Event management	3	2
Incident management	4	3
Change management	5	3
Problem management	3	1
Release and deployment management	5	3
Service asset and configuration management	5	2
Request fulfilment	3	3
IT operations management	4	3
Service level management	5	2
Service catalogue management	4	1
Service validation and testing	3	1

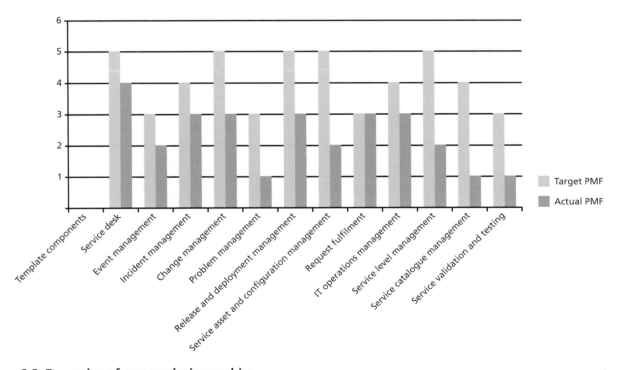

Figure 6.6 Examples of gap analysis graphics

- The costs of the workload required by staff to action and complete the plan, including the cost of any external consultants. If you will be using external consultants then you should involve them in creating the plan.
- The total potential costs of any technology required to close the gap, including the costs of updates and upgrades to other technologies to accommodate the costs of the new or updated technology. This applies to new technology or upgrades to existing technology; simply, the total costs of all technology required to complete the plan. If you anticipate having one technology solution for more than one component you will have to allocate a portion of that cost here.

The cost of education and training for the plan must also be included here.

- **Distribute your component action plan** Obtain authority to progress with your action plan for this component, or create all of the plans for all of your template components and submit them for approval together, as one plan. If your plan and its costs are approved then you can proceed, if not more work will be required to reach an agreement.
- **Finalize your component action plan** Once you have obtained feedback and taken any necessary action, finalize your plan and prepare for implementation.

You would need to repeat all of these steps even for those components that meet or exceed their target maturity levels because, when findings are distributed, different options may be aired. If your organization is already using a maturity modelling framework then you should use the gap analysis method approved by that framework.

6.5 THE MASTER ACTION PLAN

It is now time to consolidate all the information covered so far and turn it in to a well-structured action plan. Although, ideally, project management would be used, if it is not available the project can proceed using action plans. Figure 6.7 shows how an action plan is assembled.

There are three main inputs into the action master plan:

- **Defects identified as a result of gap analysis** When you performed the gap analysis you should have identified the actions required to close the gaps between the target maturity levels and the actual maturity levels.
- **ITIL publications, education and guidance** Ensure that you have the ITIL publications and any relevant complementary guides to hand. This is an ongoing requirement; make sure that you keep up to date with education, trade conferences and vendor events.
- **Preparation work (from this publication)** This publication offers guidance in a structured and logical manner and can be used as a reference source when creating your master action plan.

These inputs tend to be organic. They are ongoing and in need of continual checking, not one-off activities. The lower half of Figure 6.7 shows a simplified version of the action master plan structure and its associated component action plans. Remember that there needs to be one component action plan for each component.

The ITIL Lite master action plan (see Figure 6.8) can be produced using a spreadsheet and is easy to update and distribute. The concept of the master action plan schematic is that you can see the overall status of the ITIL Lite project at a glance.

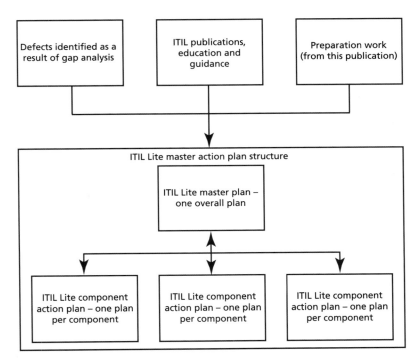

Figure 6.7 ITIL Lite master action plan structure

The master action plan is designed to be a central control point for all of the components that have been created in the component action plans.

As you can see from Figure 6.8, the master action plan looks very similar to the component action plans, and it is created in a similar way:

■ **Decide upon the resource for your master action plan** You will have decided upon the resource when you created your component action plan. Unless you have special technologies available, a spreadsheet is an inexpensive method.

■ **Decide how to integrate your master action plan with your component action plans** The master action plan gives an overall view of the project, while the component action plans give the detailed view. Ideally, you want your master action plan to be automatically updated whenever your component action plans are. Figure 6.9 shows how the individual component plans feed into the master action plan. Find a method to integrate the component action plans with the master action plan so that the master is updated every time a component is.

■ **Decide upon the contents of your master action plan** Decide upon the contents that you want to include in your master action plan – Figure 6.8 is an example. In section 6.3 we looked at the contents of a component action plan and made suggestions for extra columns. Likewise, extra columns can be added to the master action plan to make it more efficient. Do not hesitate to get advice from experienced colleagues such as project managers.

■ **Design your master action plan** Design your master action plan, keeping in mind the ability to total columns and rows. If you are using a spreadsheet use the first page of the workbook so that you can easily and quickly view the status of the master action plan.

■ **Distribute your master action plan** Before finalizing your master action plan layout you should distribute it and use any feedback to improve its contents and layout. This is an important step because we want this layout to be the best that it can. Be sure to distribute it widely and proactively gather feedback.

■ **Finalize your master action plan** Gather all of the feedback and finalize the layout and structure of your master action plan.

ITIL Lite master action plan

Owner_____ Target start date_____ Actual start date_____

Target end date_____ Actual end date_____

Version number_____ Version date_____

Component	Category	Maturity level		Workload in hours	Expenditure	Start date	End date	Percentage complete
		Actual	Target					
Service desk	A	4	5	200	£20,000	1/May/12	28/June/12	30%
Event management	A	2	3	30	£3,000	5/May/12	10/May/12	100%

More components

Figure 6.8 ITIL Lite master action plan

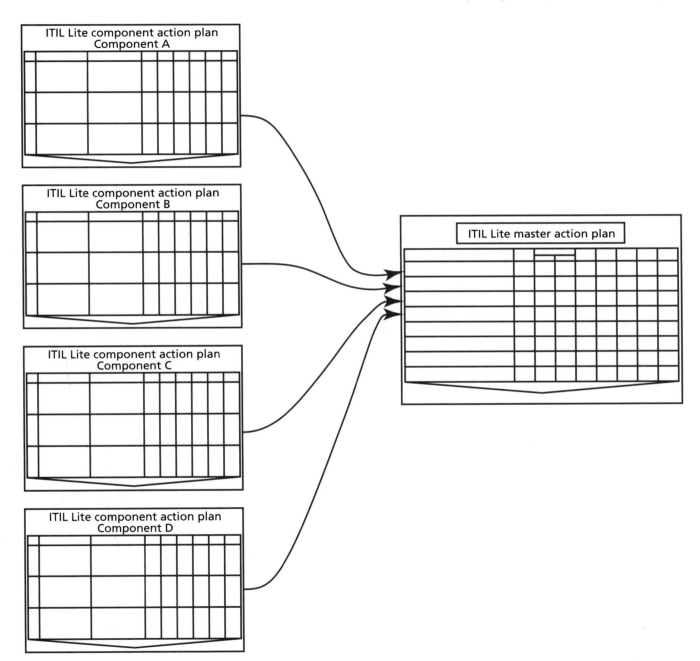

Figure 6.9 Master and component plan integration

If you have been following the planning stages you should now have your master action plan completed and fully integrated with your component action plans. The actions needed to remove the defects can now be performed and the ITIL Lite project implemented using the master and component action plans to manage the progress.

When performing actions, new defects or issues will often be uncovered. This is to be expected and, if new issues are not encountered, then it may be necessary to carry out further analysis and update action plans accordingly.

6.5.1 Managing the action plan

Now you can put your plan into action. This can be achieved following a sequence of 15 logical steps:

- **Step 1 – complete the activities described in this publication** The activities that have been described form important preparation work. They include:
  - Process design
  - Monitoring ITIL processes
  - Building ITIL Lite processes
  - Categorizing ITIL components
  - Filtering components
  - Creating ITIL Lite templates
  - Deciding component maturity
  - Prioritizing components
  - Gap analysis.

  All of these activities should be completed before work on the action plan begins.

- **Step 2 – appoint a master action plan manager** The master action plan manager is responsible for controlling the action plan and is expected to get the action plan completed on time and within budget. Ideally, the master action plan

manager would have some planning or project control skills. This is an important role because the success of the whole action plan depends largely upon the person in this position. The master action plan manager is also responsible for regularly reviewing the component action plans to ensure that they are being carried out to meet deadlines and budgets. Any anomalies must be reviewed and solved by the master action plan manager. If there is a manager to control all of the activities described in step 1 then this person would be the logical person to take on this role.

- **Step 3 – appoint the component action plan owners** The component action plan owners are responsible for controlling their action plans and are expected to get their own action plans completed on time and within budget. Ideally, the component action plan owners would have some skills that relate to their components (e.g. some related capacity experience to handle the capacity management component). This is an important position because the success of the component action plans rests with the people given this role. The component action plan owners are also responsible for updating the relevant fields in the master action plan at regular intervals. In addition, the component action plan owners must immediately report any anomalies that may appear.

- **Step 4 – component action plan owners to identify defects** Gap analysis should have identified many of the defects already, so the main role of the component action plan owners at this point is to review the defects that have been identified and add any additional ones that need to be resolved to ensure that maturity levels can be met. At this point, the component action plan owners should reassess the defects with the master action plan manager to ensure that the correct defects have been included in their component action plans. The master action plan manager will then give permission to work on the next stage, which is to identify the actions that need to be taken.

- **Step 5 – component action plan owners to identify activities** With the defects agreed, it is now time to identify the actions that must be taken to eliminate those defects. To do this, the component action plan owners need to identify the actions, the workload and the cost (of any other technologies and other expenditures). Here, the component action plan owners should reassess the actions with the master action plan manager to ensure that the correct actions have been included in the component action plans and that the required expenditure is available – although this may take some negotiating. In some cases, there may be more than one action required to eliminate a defect. In this case you have to decide whether the component action plan owners select the appropriate action or whether the master action plan owner makes the decision.

- **Step 6 – component action plan owners to complete component action plan forms** Component action plan owners should now have all the data that they require to complete the component action plan forms. The defects/ actions should be entered on the spreadsheet in the priority order that has already been decided.

- **Step 7 – component action plan owners to update the master action plan** Once they have updated the component action plans, the component action plan owners can total the appropriate columns and then update their entries in the master action plans.

- **Step 8 – plans to be approved** At this point the master action plan manager, for the first time, should have the complete scope of the project and, as a result, can present it to senior management for approval and funding. This may mean some changes to the component action plans but, at the end of this step, the project should have authority to continue.

- **Step 9 – component action plan owners to start work on their component action plans** The component action plan owners can now start working on implementing the actions that have been specified in their component action plans and authorized by the master action plan manager. The order in which the actions are to be processed should have already been decided and this order should be followed here. Any anomalies discovered when implementing the actions must be reported to the master action plan manager immediately.

- **Step 10 – component action plan owners periodically update their action plans** The master action plan manager should tell the component action plan owners how often they need to update their action plans, e.g. weekly or monthly.

- **Step 11 – component action plan owners periodically update the master action plan** The master action plan manager should set a timetable for the component action plan owners to update the master action plan. Once the timetable has been set, the component action plan owners should gather the necessary data from their component action plans and update the master action plan accordingly.

- **Step 12 – master action plan manager reviews the master action plan** As and when the master action plan is updated, the master action plan manager must review it to ensure that it is meeting its target deadlines.

- **Step 13 – issues from the master and component action plans are reviewed and addressed** If the previous step identified any issues or anomalies the master action plan manager should address them here. This may mean going back to an earlier step (e.g. step 5 – component action plan owners to identify activities) to resolve the issue.

- **Step 14 – close each component action plan as it ends** The component action plan owners should total each component action plan as it comes to its conclusion. The component action plan owners should also produce a component action plan summary and present it to the master action plan manager.

- **Step 15 – wrap up the master action plan** The master action plan manager should total the plan as soon as the last component action plan is completed. The master action plan manager should also produce a master action plan summary and present it to senior management.

The length of the master action plan differs greatly from one organization to the next but what is certain is that the plan requires skill and diligence if it is to be successful.

Summary 7

7 Summary

7.1 EXAMPLE ROAD MAP

This publication can be used as a road map to plot and manage an ITIL Lite implementation project (see Figure 7.1). You can see that the ITIL Lite road map has been divided into three classic stages – pre-planning, planning and implementation. The objective of the pre-planning stage is to ensure that the requirements of an ITIL Lite implementation are read and understood by all relevant people.

IT and ITSM planners can read this publication to decide whether ITIL Lite should be included in future long-term plans; ITSM managers can read it to review the scope of ITIL Lite implementation and determine which parts of the publication should be included in the building of an ITIL Lite initiative; and the project leader can read it to judge how it could assist in the creation of an ITIL Lite project. When these key people have read this publication they should confer to synchronize and document their requirements.

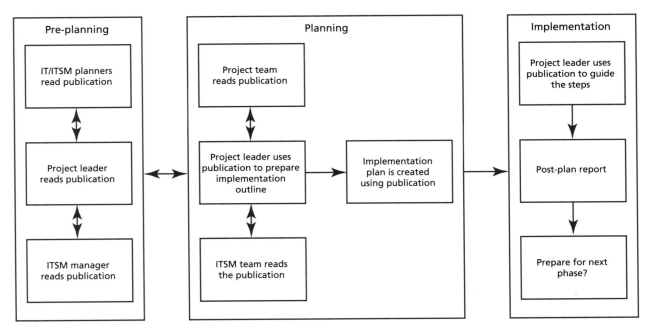

Figure 7.1 ITIL Lite road map

Once the pre-planning requirements have been documented, the project team should read this publication to support and focus the creation of an ITIL Lite project. Likewise, the ITSM team should read it to ensure that they are familiar with the logic and lessons it contains. After conferring with the project and ITSM team, and once they have read the publication, the project leader should create a draft implementation outline. This should then be circulated with a request for feedback from all of the other participants – IT/ITSM planners, the ITSM manager, ITSM team members and the project team. Once feedback has been collated the project leader, along with the project team, can create the ITIL Lite project. It is strongly recommended that a project management best practice, such as PRINCE2, is used.

7.2 CONTINUAL IMPROVEMENT

Once implemented, ITIL Lite should be continually reviewed to determine whether any new ITIL components need to be added. Sometimes this happens organically and the statistics produced by the implemented components point to the need for another component, or components, to be implemented or improved. If so, the steps in this publication need to be repeated to ensure that the components are properly implemented. Sometimes, the category for a component may have changed, a non-ITIL component is hindering ITIL, or other functions (such as governance) are being compromised. Whatever the reason, ITIL Lite requires constant vigilance to stay fully effective. In other words, apply continual service improvement principles.

The journey starts rather than ends here.

Index

Index